A GOD OF SECOND CHANCES

*A Guide to Reclaiming
God's Call on Our Lives*

JOHN & JERRI DOCTOR

A GOD OF SECOND CHANCES
– A Guide to Reclaiming God's Call on Our Lives

Copyright © 2017 John & Jerri Doctor

Published by
Broken Vessel Publishing

All Scripture quotations, unless otherwise indicated, are taken from the Holy Bible, New International Version®, NIV®. Copyright ©1973, 1978, 1984, 2011 by Biblica, Inc.™ Used by permission of Zondervan. All rights reserved worldwide. www.zondervan.com The "NIV" and "New International Version" are trademarks registered in the United States Patent and Trademark Office by Biblica, Inc.™

ISBN: 978-0-9992354-0-9

Library of Congress Control Number: 2017951386

Printed in the United States of America

To reach the authors, go to:

www.aGodOfSecondChances.org

ABOUT THE COVER

Kintsukuroi (金繕い) (Japanese: golden repair) is the Japanese art of repairing broken pottery with lacquer mixed with powdered gold, silver, or platinum.

Typically, the broken pottery was common and simple when it was broken, but it becomes more beautiful and more valuable because of the repair.

In the same way, through the gift of second chances, God can turn a broken life into one of great beauty and value.

Dear Father, Mother, My Creator, Creator
Divine
Help me to Be able to
reintegrate the Damage caused Cost to
The Beautiful, Pure, Ethereal
Body that I was gifted by
You two. Help me on this
Journey to use every tool.
resource needed to stay
In Constant Communication
with You two, So my little
Lego (monsta) doesn't try

WHAT OTHERS ARE SAYING

Without question, John and Jerri are reflecting to the world a facet of God's character. It is a delight to see, not only because it is 100% true, but because it is 100% on target. We need to be reminded afresh of God's unending desire to love us back to wholeness. That is one of the many things He does so well.

> – Brian Mast, author of *Know Love, Live Loved*
> Publisher, Author Pool Founder

A God of Second Chances is a great resource for everyone who has endured life's pains and struggles. John and Jerri Doctor are great examples themselves of the Lord bringing beauty from ashes. This book is filled with insight and wisdom from God in learning from our past but moving forward with healing and hope. I have known this couple for many years and know they live what they teach.

> – Pastor Dave Folkerts
> Associate Pastor, Calvary Chapel Melbourne, FL

Romans 3:23 declares three catastrophic words, "all have sinned" while 2 Corinthians 12:9 announces the four-word contrast, "My grace is sufficient." John and Jerri Doctor capture this supernatural truth by leading readers to embrace their current circumstances in *A God of Second Chances*. Expect their words to transform your heart to a meaningful life of ministry.

> – Debbie Browne
> Author, *Loving a Leaping Butterfly*
> Founder and CEO, Leaping Butterfly Ministry

My friends, John and Jerri, know from personal experience the power of God to rebuild broken worlds. I am confident that God will use their words to breathe hope into healed hearts. This book answers the question: God, what's my next move now that I am back strong?

– Mark Ragsdale
Senior Pastor, Church at Viera, Viera, Florida

to keep me from growing, &
expanding & Re-claiming my
place within Our interconnected
web ~~with infinite eternal~~
Be God/Goddess Humanity seeking to
vessels for ~~reclaiming~~ reclaiming Our inner
Divinity so You too can
share in Bring You, Our
Lord Light. and Creator, to
Our Mother & Your bride
Sophia Creatrix - Goddess
of Compassion, & Being Beauty
+ Being All that good in the world

DEDICATION

We dedicate this book

>...first and foremost, to the Lord, who healed our past and has restored our dreams;
>...to our mentors, Rundle & Cinda Smith and Steve Whitemarsh, who inspired and believed in us;
>...and to you, the reader, who yearn to reclaim God's call on your life.

May We all Learn to reconcile our differences & allow every human, & living Being to Do the part they came here to play. Amen

Julie

PREFACE

The concept of law and gospel, sin and grace, repentance and forgiveness has been the heart of Christian teaching since the Church's inception in Jerusalem. To this day, faithful churches teach on "...Word made Flesh..." in Jesus Christ. Truly alive and dynamic churches teach that the real goal is not simply a knowledge of who God [Father, Son (Jesus), and Holy Spirit] is, but to have a relationship with Him. What we seek to teach here has its roots in both God's grace and a relationship with Him.

The Christian Church has always, through preaching and teaching, confronted sin and offered grace. The church has also provided help, comfort, and counsel to those who have suffered loss or who are hurting. The modern church has established many support programs: divorce recovery, chemical dependency, grief counseling, job/career loss, and even physical health and diet assistance, all to help those who suffered the loss of their "first" opportunity." So now, when we have healed and God says, "It's time for you to try again," what do we do?

This book picks up where the support programs have left off. The study is designed to help people determine why they have been given a second chance and give them the tools to hear from God what they are to do with it. This is not to say that everyone who "completes" one of the help or healing programs needs to immediately advance into this material or that going through a program is a prerequisite for this process. Rather, this book is for people who have healed, however long that takes, and may well sense a new call on their lives or even just a feeling that they don't need to maintain the status quo any more.

We realize that God is much more than a "God of second chances," and each person's situation is unique. God most often

[handwritten annotations] God, This pain + suffering keep getting worse — So this is someone who doesn't — is need any help, they're already healed. Duh!!

gives us many chances, as we live in His grace and seek to obey Him. It is also important for us to state that, although our own sinful behavior may frequently be at the root of our life-changing crisis, not all crises are the result of our personal sinful behavior.

For a second chance to be successful, certain healing and understanding must take place. When we are unprepared for a second chance, we run the risk of its failure. If we do fail, we may consciously or subconsciously torpedo future chances: the person who sabotages a new relationship or undermines an interview derails opportunities in order to avoid being vulnerable and failing, often without even understanding what they are doing or why. It could be even more overt: the person who mishandles an opportunity may make a conscious choice to "never to get into that situation again." Their fear and lack of faith lead to permanent failure by preventing another attempt.

Cop out

CONTENTS

INTRODUCTION

Second chances are new beginnings. A chance to close the door to past hurts, failures, disappointments, and broken dreams as well as the shame, rejection, or embarrassment that may come with them.

Humbled by the opportunity given, by God's hand, and the fact that I don't deserve it makes me want to look around as I step onto the stage of a new chapter in my life. I step out, half expecting disparaging "boo's" and accusatory tomatoes to be thrown by an audience filled with the tailored suits and starched flowered dresses of my past wrongdoings.

I am surprised and greatly relieved to find there is no one there in the audience but My Father, God, who looks beyond all that I see and (He) smiles. He sees something inside me that He loves. I'm sure I don't see what He does, but I am very grateful there is love and a fresh start.

I want to share with you, the reader, how He speaks of reconciliation, how He speaks of second chances – how He speaks of beauty for ashes:

> "To appoint unto them that mourn in Zion, to give unto them beauty for ashes, the oil of joy for mourning, the garment of praise for the spirit of heaviness; that they might be called trees of righteousness, the planting of the LORD, that he might be glorified." (Isaiah 61:3 KJV)

And how He creates a valuable piece of artwork when we give Him the broken pieces of our lives.

– Jerri D.

House of Broken Dreams (by Jerri)

The road was long with twisted fate
Dead trees remained with broken gate
The doors ajar the roof torn down
The rich green hopes had turned all brown

I found myself with broken thoughts
What hopes and plans were never wrought
A graveyard filled with dreams gone by
Of passions, plays and things that died

And in the distance dark clouds shake
As if to answer my mistakes
It is the Lord who paves the way
And offers me a brand-new day

A star so small; His great expanse
He offers me a second chance
I take a breath and bow my heart
In gratefulness – Another start.

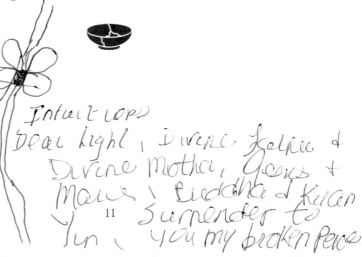

Infinite Lords
Dear Light, Divine Father &
Divine Mother, Jesus &
Mary, Buddha & Kuan
Yin, you my broken Peace
Surrender to

11

CHAPTER ONE

A LOST FIRST

On any given day at any given time someone experiences loss. The economy goes south, jobs are eliminated, and people forfeit their homes or have to move. This causes them to leave their community of friends, churches, schools, and daycares they love.

In 2012 alone, over 51 million Americans lost their jobs; there were 2.5 million deaths, and about half of all marriages ended in divorce.

It is estimated that 45% of all U.S. jobs will be automated within the next 20 years; half the current workforce could lose their employment status due to technology and automation, not to mention those which may be affected by the economy.

Loss is a reality we have to deal with.

Although this book is about second chances, the very title itself implies that there must have been a first chance. Moreover, that first chance was lost, either through failure, missed opportunity, or crisis, which created the need for a second chance. These losses can be devastating and leave us hopeless. But the grace of God can give us a second chance to live a fulfilled life.

In order to succeed at a second chance, we must first understand a loss.

What Is Loss?

A loss is the fact or process of surrendering something or someone against our will and the resulting state of grief. It, by nature, suggests that you had something to start with, but somehow you no longer have it. Loss is also inevitable in this life.

While the physical, tangible aspects of loss may be overwhelming, there are other aspects of loss as well. The package of loss includes feelings and emotions. These emotions are strong and varied and may progress from a temporary state of sorrow, grief, rejection, despair, loneliness, and shame to a more permanent sense of failure, worthlessness, embarrassment, hopelessness, abandonment, emptiness, and devastation.

While physical and emotional effects are more obvious, a significant element frequently overlooked is that there is a spiritual side to loss. We are made in the likeness of God, which means that we are more than a body and a mind. The Bible identifies us as being made up of three parts: body, soul, and spirit. Our bodies are the physical, tangible part of who we are; our souls are the seat of our emotions and feeling; and our spirit is the source of our identity and our connection with God.

Whatever the proportion, recognition, or value we give these different aspects of ourselves, they are an undeniable part of who we are. Spiritual loss creates in us the sense of separation between God and ourselves. Just as physical and emotional loss can be measured, the impact on your spirit can result in the loss of your dreams, hopes, desires, and plans for your future. Broken spirits can be caused by (or result in) broken vows and unkept promises. The loss becomes intricately woven into a person's very matrix.

When our foundational beliefs are rocked or shattered, we can find ourselves grasping at the ledges of life itself. What happened? What do I do now? What comes next? Who am I? All of these things speak to the core of our very spirit being and will not be dismissed lightly.

We have all experienced loss. Yet it is possible to face those hardships and come out miraculously intact. Some people are empowered by circumstances that would dissolve others. They bounce back into society and continue their life more vigorously than before. The strength I see in people who have faced such horrible things is amazing beyond words.

The significance of loss is subjective. One person may lose a job and happily go out and find another; a second person may lose a job and his self-esteem with it, and be paralyzed. One may view the loss of a pet as a non-emotional event in the cycle of life; another may perceive it as devastating as the loss of a child. And then there are times when someone faces a loss and just can't recover. What is the difference? Why can't some of us just seem to "snap out of it"? And now comes the big question: is it even healthy for a person just to "snap out of it"?

While physical and emotional effects are more obvious, a significant element frequently overlooked is that there is a spiritual side to loss.

How we react to loss is in some ways tied to how many times we have faced loss. Experiencing loss changes how we react to future losses. Either we adapt by shielding or hardening, or we can become weaker.

How we cope, the number of coping tools we have at our disposal, and the armor we have are all affected by the number of times we have had to use them. We may have faced many losses in our lives, yet there may come a day when ONE more loss is all it takes to push us over the edge. Instead of being able to cope successfully, overcome as before, and move on, we get stuck or even decline into an unhealthy state – whether it is mentally, physically, or spiritually centered.

Some of this depends on our matrix: where we came from, the lessons learned as a child, and who our role models were. There is neither a formula nor reproducible factors in any given person that ensures success or failure to cope as compared to another. We may have the "perfect" set of parents and be raised in a world of more than adequate circumstances and surroundings yet grow up unable to face a crisis and "come out of it."

Regardless of how we respond and how long it takes us to recover – we have all experienced a loss.

Sometimes a loss is unavoidable. Sometimes we see it coming. Other times it is sudden, unexpected. Sometimes we will be prepared and other times there will be no preparation. No matter what the circumstances or our level of preparedness, loss will make an impact on us and will change our perspective on life and our future.

Major vs. Minor Loss

The list of possible losses is almost endless. My only reason for listing some of them is to get people to think outside of the box and realize that loss can take many forms. Moreover, losses that may seem less significant than others can have the same or even greater impact on our lives due to our efforts to hide or minimize them. If something or someone is important to you, its loss will have an impact.

Loss, for the purposes of this discussion, can be divided into two categories: critical losses and subtle losses. But regardless of the severity of the loss, what we do with our feelings can help or hurt our healing process.

The first category includes those which are most commonly understood as "major" by our culture. The loss of a loved one through death and the loss of a marriage through death or divorce are probably the first two events that come to mind when we talk about loss in our culture. While these are no doubt among the most visible, the loss of a job and/or loss of finances (i.e., bankruptcy) can be every bit as common and have as great an impact as a death. This is especially true today, as so many people define their identity by their occupation. The loss of a job challenges their identity, even if they are voluntarily leaving a job due to retirement. And financial collapse and ruined credit calls into question how people survive in a cash- or credit-driven society.

Another common loss is illness that takes away freedom of movement or other physical ability. But what we might not consider is the disfigurement that may be caused by the illness or injury. The loss of our appearance often creates a loss of our self-confidence. In II Corinthians 12, the apostle Paul speaks of his struggles with a "thorn in the flesh," which – although Paul never clearly defines what that issue was – many scholars believe was a physical condition that caused some form of disfigurement. Paul was never relieved of this "thorn" and had to learn to live with it, which he did by the power of Christ Jesus whose "strength was made perfect in (my) weakness."

We, too, may have to come to terms with some form of permanent disfigurement as the result of a health issue. This loss could go back to our childhood or even be an issue from birth.

The loss of a friend can have a huge impact on us. The loss may be the result of death or relocation, but it often is the result of an argument (and pride). Although the latter can be corrected through humbleness and repentance, the scars from the hurt can remain for the rest of the friendship. A trust that is lost is not easily restored. Even the loss of your temper that in some way has cost you a relationship or the respect that others had for you is a form of loss.

The friends we lose are not always human. The loss of a long-time family pet can be emotionally devastating. The loss is so acute because it takes with it the fierce loyalty and unconditional love that the animal gives to us.

The last of the common major losses are the results of change. You don't really do without, but what you have is different from what you had. The change of a job or position (even a promotion) moves you from what you know to something that is unfamiliar to you. A move from a new neighborhood or city can include a change of churches. This can be especially difficult when you are leaving a close church family and an established place in ministry for a place where no one knows you, and you have to reestablish your role through basic involvement.

Minor losses are much subtler. In fact, you may not always see them as losses when they occur. Years later, you realize the effect these events have had on you, and only then do you recognize them as losses. These could include the incremental loss of your senses and/or your memory as a natural result of aging. A changing culture as our world leaves behind the norms that made you feel secure – even growing ethnic diversity of your community – can be experienced as a loss of your heritage and the way of life that you grew up with. The loss of youth can be a very serious issue for some.

> No matter what the circumstances or our level of preparedness, loss will make an impact on us and will change our perspective on life and our future.

Subtle losses may include the loss of a goal or dream that you once believed was possible but now have accepted is out of your reach: the child who dreamed of being an athlete but lacks the ability; the business person who dreamed of being a CEO but retires in middle management; the musician who dreamed of being a star but makes a living playing for weddings or community events; and the couple who dreamed of being parents but finds they are infertile. All of these people are dreamers who have lost their dream. Although some will take it harder than others, the loss of our dreams affects us all.

Some dreams are not possible; however, loss of those dreams carries the potential for the loss of our goals as well. Since goals motivate us, the loss of a goal (even by fulfilling it) can affect our very motivation and cause us to struggle, though we may not understand why we are struggling.

One of the most devastating losses that can occur to someone is the loss of morals or ethics, subtle because it occurs slowly, over time. It starts with a little compromise of personal values and then grows until one day they realize that they've traded integrity for convenience and virtue for passions. In an effort to achieve our goals, we may justify the compromises as necessary evils. It is the parents who sacrifice time with their children to get ahead at work because they are "doing it to make our family better off." It is the singles who compromise their sexual purity to "keep from losing the love of their life." It is the people who distort the truth or use others to achieve their goals because "I know what is best for everyone and I need to make sure that it happens."

Because our ethics influence so much of our lives, their loss can have a massive effect. Additionally, due to the nature of time, we can never go back and undo what we have done or retrieve precisely what we have lost. But this is where the grace of God is our one hope! Here is where God's love shines through. He does not undo the loss we experience, but He helps us to overcome the effect of the loss, gives us the ability to rebuild our lives, and empowers us to take hold of our future.

What is your loss or vulnerability to loss? Listening to how you would describe yourself to someone else will give you a pretty good idea of your greatest vulnerability. Good or bad, whatever character trait, skill, relationship, position, heritage, or possession you include in your description is probably a "value" to you and something you will struggle with if lost.

Some things are best taught by experience. Our (the authors') personal losses have been significant. We have experienced both personal and corporate loss, both as individuals and together.

In particular, the untimely death of a parent, as well as the murder of a sibling and a shattered family at an early age, tore away Jerri's foundation of safety and stability and challenged her faith and ability to find security in life.

John has faced the loss of his career which challenged his calling and created the need to reinvent himself many times. This included a prolonged period of unemployment following a failed business startup attempt early in our new marriage.

Both of us experienced the loss of a first marriage. That led each of us to question ourselves, especially our value and purpose in life. It left us vulnerable, without hope for any future intimate relationship.

Out of these losses, God revealed to us the power and opportunity of His grace in "Second Chances."

The First Consequence of Sin

It wasn't always like this. The Bible teaches us that, from the beginning, God created man in His image: perfect in every way. Being created in His image meant that our will was equal to – the same as – God's will for us. We understood naturally God's call on our life and desire for us. It also left room for creativity and uniqueness. Therefore, we had a perfect comprehension of that which was good, "God Good."

Part of God's perfect plan was the gift of choice. Genesis teaches us that when God created the Garden of Eden, He placed in it, among everything else, a certain tree. This tree contained within its fruit the knowledge of "Good" and "Evil." Why was this tree planted in the Garden? Since we were created in God's image, we already had the knowledge of God's Good; therefore, this tree could only bring the knowledge of evil and a skewed "good," – as defined by the world – that would flow from the release of its knowledge.

Why would God bring such a dangerous opportunity into His perfect creation? In His love, He has given mankind freedom of choice. God values choice. It was not enough that God had created us and that we were bound to Him as our Creator; He wanted us to choose Him as our Lord, to serve and obey Him of our own accord.

The tree introduced to humanity the knowledge of evil and corrupted "good." The result was the appearance of the sin of pride, which had only been seen once in the heavenly realm when Satan rebelled and was cast out of heaven. It introduced the desire to be equal to God, and it actually preceded the act of eating the fruit. Thus, forever, man would be robbed of his innocence by his lust to be like God.

Let's look at eight things we have lost as the result of mankind's fall into sin:

1. Loss of innocence
2. Loss of a relationship with God
3. Loss of purity
4. Loss of peace
5. Loss of immortality
6. Loss of trust
7. Loss of ease of life
8. Loss of the knowledge of good

Innocence

A baby can be stripped down and put into a swimming pool and think nothing of it ... but wait five years and the same child would be embarrassed and ashamed at being naked.

There was a very significant loss that is sometimes minimized in the story of the fall of Adam and Eve. This was the very first act of a deliberate shedding of blood. Let us explain.

Prior to this event, there was no death. As we read in Genesis, once Adam and Eve realized their nakedness (loss of innocence), they sought to cover themselves with fig leaves. But this was a temporary, short-sighted action from beings who did not understand the full significance of the loss that had just occurred.

God understood that there was more at stake than just the knowledge of being naked. He understood that we would never again, on our own, be able to see the good and perfect will of God uncontaminated by the knowledge of evil. Therefore, He clothed their nakedness with an animal's skin gained through sacrificing of life. The covering of their shame came with a price, paid by the animal. The leaf was not enough. The wool from a sheep was not enough. It required the sacrifice of innocent life, with one life given because of what another had done. It was a foreshadowing of our need to be clothed with the ultimate sacrifice of Christ in order to regain innocence.

Relationship with God

By their sin, Adam and Eve were separated from God. They immediately hid from Him. When we sin (and try to hide it) we build walls that isolate us from our Creator. By distancing ourselves, we create a false sense of independence. Inasmuch as God is perfect, the introduction of sin contaminated us and no longer allowed us to come into His holy presence uncovered. Relationship with Him was lost. No longer does our knowledge of good dominate our thoughts, our lives. The evil that we know separates us from God's character.

Although our conscience bears witness to the existence of God, we no longer have innate understanding of WHO God is. As a result, though there are few cultures that espouse a belief in atheism, there are numerous efforts to define who God is through many different religions. Left on our own, we will never find the true God; we lost that relationship. The only way to restore it is through His son.

> "I am the way and the truth and the life. No one comes to the Father except through me." (John 14:6)

Purity

The loss of purity isn't from fruit to myriad impure things, because even before Adam and Eve ate the fruit they had already sacrificed purity by giving in to the desire to be like God (Genesis 3:5). That surrender was the beginning of a war that would last all man's days on the earth. We now fight the battle of the mind, fighting off constant temptation, the evil desires that our sinful nature wishes to pursue. In our corrupt state, we would never again know who God is without external intervention.

Peace

Peace comes from confidence in who you are, what you are to do, where it is to take you, and the certainty that you have the ability to do it. Once sin entered into the picture, we were robbed of that very assurance. The use of the fig leaf and its failure to provide covering was the first evidence that we did not have the ability to be what we were made to be or do what we are called to do on our own. Therefore, peace was lost.

Immortality

When God said of His creation "it is good," death played no part. It was only through the contamination of sin that total separation from the life God provides entered the world. Perfection cannot tolerate impurity. Therefore, impurity must be separated and eliminated. Thus, death was the natural consequence of and penalty for sin. Death not only refers to the loss of physical life, but far more importantly, it describes the loss of eternal life. Sin brought with it a total separation from God. But God chose to bridge the gap of eternal separation through His son Jesus.

There is another condition that came with the curse of death – disease, injury, aging, and death would now be a natural part of our existence. Seeing this consequence of sin, God also removed access to the Tree of Life, lest we live forever in this corrupted state.

Trust

When the serpent lied, mankind heard a lie for the first time. We were deceived. When we no longer have the ability to distinguish the truth from a lie, trust is lost. We lost the ability to trust God naturally. Without trust, we developed cynicism and doubt. We simply stopped believing that what God says is true. Moreover, we struggle at simply recognizing God's voice when He speaks to us.

Additionally, the natural knowledge of God's truth was lost. Mankind has since been wracked with the innate desire to know who God is, tormented by the confusion of carnal philosophy and logic, desperately trying to understand God through scientific thinking, which attempts to subject God to the natural laws He assigned to man. We are born with a vacuum: a desire to know God. And we are forever trying to fill that void with self-made gods that come in all sizes and wear many faces. Without a clear knowledge of truth, we have lost the confidence that comes with trust.

Ease of Life

Weeds, work, and worry are now constants in our lives. We eat by the sweat of our brow and bear childbirth in pain. Just as the weeds of sin entered the perfect garden of God, so also weeds now populate every aspect of our lives.

> Crisis is the result of how we react to loss, not the loss itself.

Weeds are not just unwanted plants – weeds are unwanted thoughts, unanticipated circumstances, unintended results. Weeds of discontentment, jealousy, envy, and resentment plague us on a daily basis. They can rob us of our hopes, aspirations, dreams, and sense of purpose. The most frustrating thing of all about these weeds is that you don't have to plant them; they appear on their own, even if you do nothing. Thus, we will always have to work at life. Tied to loss of peace, the ease of a perfect relationship with our Creator has been replaced with a perpetual striving with God.

Knowledge of Good

At the root of all of this chaos is the loss of the natural knowledge of God's Good. We no longer have a perfect knowledge of moral and ethical behavior. In an interim sense, it created a need for the Ten Commandments, The Law, and punishment for disobeying the law. Not only was the knowledge of Good destroyed, but the introduction of sin became an all-consuming knowledge.

The Relationship of Loss and Crisis

Again, for a second chance to occur, a first loss must happen. There is more to loss than just what we lost. How we lose something also becomes a factor in healing and being ready for a second chance. The circumstances that cause loss may be very passive and progress over time; others are sudden and quite traumatic. Traumatic loss is something that many would describe as a crisis. Some people may assume that loss and crisis are the same, but crisis is not the same as loss.

It is very common to see two people face similar losses and one to come unglued and the other to take a deep breath and move on. Why is that? Crisis is the result of how we react to loss, not the loss itself. Crises may happen to the same person who has successfully overcome a loss in the past. How we react is influenced by a great many things – especially our spiritual health, our mental health, and our physical health – and these things change in our lives over time.

Our well-being is a platform for our reactions. If we have faced one too many stressors that year, a crisis may become *the straw that broke the camel's back*. We may have been blindsided and simply unprepared for the emotional impact of an event; had we had time to prepare, it might have affected us differently. It could be that we have suffered a physical ailment, and most of our energy is utilized in coping with chronic pain. It could also be that we have slipped from a position of intimacy with the Lord and we ourselves have been the driving force of self-sufficiency. We are no longer dependent on God until there is something bigger than our limited resources can handle.

We can overcome crises by learning how to effectively and positively react to loss. That involves accepting the fact that loss has occurred, so as to be able to heal from the hurt. It includes learning from our experiences in order to avoid the danger of repeating the failure or a crisis reaction to it. Losses are inevitable, but growth is optional.

In a time of instability, we must find something stable and constant. The only constant we have in our world is God. His love is unchanging.

> "The counsel of the LORD stands forever, the plans of His heart from generation to generation." (Psalm 33:11)

"For I, the LORD, do not change; therefore you, O sons of Jacob, are not consumed." (Malachi 3:6)

"Jesus Christ is the same yesterday and today and forever." (Hebrews 13:8)

Only by finding the sure footing that Jesus Christ brings are we able to regain control of our emotions and be in a position to start healing.

The 5 Ds of Loss

What are the possible impacts of loss in our lives? No one comes through loss unscathed. The question is what kind of impact does it have on our lives? How do we react to it? How does it alter our view of the past? How does it shape our future? In the words of John Maxwell, "sometimes you win, sometimes you learn." To be able to learn, however, we must understand how we respond to loss. Let us consider five possible responses to loss.

D#1: Disarmed

Merriam Webster defines *disarm* as "to take weapons from (someone or something); to give up weapons; to make (a bomb, mine, etc.) harmless; to deprive of means, reason, or disposition to be hostile; to win over; to divest of arms; to deprive of a means of attack or defense; to make harmless."

To be disarmed is not to be unable to fight or cope, but to have your coping skills – your weapons – removed or otherwise unavailable for use. Some people are more vulnerable to being disarmed simply because their coping skills are less developed or they simply have fewer coping skills to start with. This could be the result of a trauma early in life, stunting the development of coping skills, or perhaps there was no role model to help in the development of these defenses.

Disarming renders you ineffective. Often, it occurs because you are naïve or unsuspecting of an impending crisis and are therefore caught off guard by the loss. Sometimes we *choose* not to see; we refuse to take into account the warning signs or accept the likely outcome of a given situation.

Even if a person has an armory of coping mechanisms which they have employed successfully in the past, sometimes there is no way to predict loss. Disarming most often occurs because of a crisis and not just a loss.

A situation that disarms us causes us to lose the ability to focus on recovery. If we do not recognize our situation and seek help, then we (the disarmed person) may become disabled.

I (Jerri) found myself disarmed as a young adult when I attempted to enter the world unprepared. At 17 years of age, I had been given the legal responsibility and granted guardianship of my elementary-aged sibling. Oh, as much as I sought to take over parental responsibilities, I had no reservoir from which to dip in some vital areas. Because of the gap in my own upbringing, I fell short of the wisdom required to parent effectively. I did not have enough of a foundational ground nor was there an adult to "mirror" or mentor my skill-set, abilities, and gifts that would assist in navigating my future, let alone prepare me to have input into someone else's.

> The only constant we have in our world is God. His love is unchanging.

I didn't give much consideration to college or career during my youth. Day-to-day survival itself was the urgent and critical demand. My family experienced a year of shell shock following my father's death. I spent the next decade ensuring that my mother was safe and trying to get help for her. Finally, I was able to attend to my own life, but I had been acting out of duty, putting out the continual fires for so long that I couldn't function any other way. I found myself using the same few coping mechanisms for every situation and eventually felt the world too big a place for me. I was unable to think in terms of developing my future. By the time I began college, anxiety and stress were already causing me physical symptoms. I was overwhelmed and felt I had little control.

D#2: Disabled

A person who is disabled is one who has become paralyzed by the trauma of their crisis. Though they may know what has happened, they lack the ability to do anything about it. The presence of coping skills is irrelevant, due to the belief that they were never able to be successful in the area of their loss. Frequently, the disabled person has suffered a loss that challenges their character, ability, and/or purpose. The nature of the loss is such that they are unable to learn from it. Like the disarmed person, the disabled person is rendered helpless to effectively manage a crisis and sometimes even everyday stressors.

Like disarming, disabling is most often the result of a crisis, rather than just a loss. Someone very dear to my heart, whom I'll call Jim, experienced a trauma as a young adult, a trauma so painful he never got over it. Saddened by the loss of another person's life, Jim assumed responsibility for that loss. The incident seared his mind and heart so deeply that he never forgave himself. He became psychologically disabled. Powerful guilt and shame set in motion a pattern of failure. Jim completed college, but without the passion that had once been a career catalyst. Failing the state board exam by a mere two points was perceived as further evidence of personal failure, which then sent him into an even deeper depression. He settled for a string of occupations and relationships that were never part of his dream.

It saddens my heart to think how many strong leaders in our homes and in our communities we have lost – not to mention those we have lost in the Kingdom of God. How many are we losing due to the lies we believe about who we are and what we can accomplish?

> "Watch your thoughts, they become words;
> watch your words, they become actions;
> watch your actions, they become habits;
> watch your habits, they become character;
> watch your character, for it becomes your destiny."
> – *Frank Outlaw, late President of Bi-Lo Stores*

D#3: Deluded

Delusion may occur as the result of being either disarmed or disabled by loss. It may also be used as a coping tool that stems from an individual's attempt to minimize the loss as "not that important," or "only temporary." Consciously or subconsciously, they have simply chosen not to cope with the loss.

A deluded person may be living in a state of denial, believing that the loss did not really happen and that somehow everything will go back to the way it was. The lack of acceptance of the loss means that no meaningful healing or progress can be made.

I saw an example of this while I was working in the state employment assistance agency in Florida. It was during the mass layoffs at the end of the Space Shuttle Program. Thousands of workers were laid off, but many of them, especially the older workers, were convinced that the decision to end the shuttle program would be reversed. Many were deluded in their belief that someone would come save them (rehire them). They were so convinced that the program would be restored that they sabotaged their own progress, self-destructing instead of moving forward.

> Like disarming, disabling is most often the result of a crisis, rather than just a loss.

The sad truth was that the space shuttles were being stripped of their vital components as soon as the last flight was completed, making it impossible to ever return the shuttles to flightworthy status. Furthermore, even if the decision was reversed, it would take a decade before another manned space flight program could resume launches from the Kennedy Space Center. Their belief that they could ever return to their jobs was unsupported by reality. Even though we spent a great deal of time and money trying to assist these people, many of them made themselves unemployable by their deluded thinking. They lost their future waiting for the "…cheese to come back," just as described in the best-seller *Who Moved My Cheese?*

D#4: Distracted

In an effort to "cope" with the loss, the distracted person becomes involved in as much as possible to "stay busy." This robs them of critical time and energy needed to heal. Regardless of how painful the healing process is, it must be faced and worked through if there is to ever be a real second chance.

Sometimes friends or family may, with good intentions, attempt to distract a person who has suffered a loss. They surround them and fill their days and nights with things to do in an effort to "protect" them from the pain and suffering associated with the loss. They think that they are helping the person, but the truth is that they are simply sweeping the pain under the rug – actually prolonging the healing process and stunting growth.

You can see this clearly in physical trauma. If we do not allow an injury to heal fully, we will not only continue to reinjure ourselves by premature activity, but we can also cause permanent damage and never gain full recovery. If a person breaks a bone and treats it with pain medication and/or "shaking it off" but never gets it reset, the bone can either heal in a deformed way or could even become infected and eventually be life-threatening.

In the same way, if we do not actively address the emotional and spiritual pain associated with our loss and allow for time to heal, then we do not ever return to a healthy emotional state or a place of mental or spiritual well-being.

D#5: Develop

The developed person is one who understands that a change has occurred and there will be no return to "the way things used to be." It might be interesting to note that there are multiple ways to handle a loss improperly, but only one way will result in a positive move toward healing and restoration. If you are willing to go through a great deal of self-examination and reflection and are willing to accept hard truths about yourself or your situation, you will grow and develop. This knowledge can improve your life in the future if you are willing to learn from your mistakes. Humility is the key to an open and pliable heart, capable of moving from hurt to health. Most critical of all, you must be willing to submit in faith to God's divine guidance, providence, and faithfulness.

> "Trust in the Lord with all your heart, and lean not on your own understanding; In all your ways acknowledge Him, and He shall direct your paths." (Proverbs 3:5-6)

In summary, it is important to note that most people, when faced with loss, will experience one or more of the first four responses – disarmed, disabled, deluded, distracted – before moving to a place of development. The problem is not experiencing any of the first four responses, but rather getting stuck there.

The developed person is one who understands that a change has occurred and there will be no return to "the way things used to be."

I think it is profitable to identify where you are, to know that you will not always be there if you are humble in spirit, willing to accept responsibility, ask for forgiveness where needed, and allow time for healing, being careful not to fill the void with temporary things. Then you will grow in character and spirit and be able to be used as God's vessel once again.

Sometimes we can't process loss alone. It is important to have a trusted friend who can encourage us, pray for us and with us, and build up our faith. But sometimes we need professional help.

For Discussion/Reflection:
- What was your "lost first"?
- Think about how it affected you. Did it disarm, disable, delude, or distract you?
- What steps of healing have you taken?
- Have you allowed your loss to develop you, and if so, how?

Prayer to identify your loss:

Heavenly Father, I come before You and lay down the loss that I have faced in my life. I understand that my life may never be the same, but that You have a plan for me, created long before I suffered loss. As I place my future in Your very capable hands, I pray that You would guide and direct my steps. Lead me to prayer partners; surround me with people who will help me along the way to develop a life most fruitful for Your glory; and prepare me for any second chances that You have purposed for me. In Jesus' name, Amen.

CHAPTER TWO

INHERITED LOSSES

In the first chapter, we discussed what loss is, examples of loss, and the impact that loss can have on a person. Frequently, losses we face are the result of our own mistakes. They are the result of flawed decisions, a lifestyle that was destructive, or things we said that we wish we could take back.

Loss may also result from decisions that were not made or actions that were not taken, but should have been. One very significant aspect of life is that it is fluid and changing. As a result, indecision becomes a decision of its own. Life is like a river flowing toward a waterfall. Our lives are a canoe in that river. We have four choices:

- We can live life with reckless abandon and paddle straight for the falls, either out of a sense of invincibility or from a conscious or subconscious desire to self-destruct.
- We can paddle against the current for as long as our strength holds out, but when our strength finally fails, we will still be swept over the falls.
- We can paddle toward the shore, out of the strong current to the calmer waters, where it will be easier – to not only survive, but also to advance against the current of life.
- We can do nothing, out of fear or indecision, and flow helplessly with the current, right to the falls.

The choice to do nothing is every bit as much a choice as any of the first three. Change is inevitable. Our choice to do nothing does not enable us to stay in the same place. It simply means that growth is taken out of our hands and the outcome of our future is left to others or to circumstances that impact our lives.

There is no question that there is a specific impact from losses that we are responsible for in our lives. Regret and guilt are the natural outcome from losses brought about by our failures. Although we will talk about this more in future chapters, it is important to acknowledge this vulnerability to understand the challenges we will face in this kind of loss.

But what about losses that come from another source? What about losses as the result of someone else's actions or inaction? What about the losses we have no control over but still bear the consequences for? This is the "Ugly Sweater Gift" that we want to address here.

Losses by Divine Allowance

It is important to note that some losses may even come as a result of an "act of nature" or God's allowance. Many books have been written to address the question: "Why does God allow bad things to happen?" I am not going to try to answer the question of why, because it is beyond us to comprehend the reasons of an all-knowing and infinite God. But I do think it is important to acknowledge this kind of loss before moving on.

Some calamities referenced in the Old Testament came about as punishment by God for the disobedience of His people in an effort to turn them back to Him. But most "natural disasters" are simply the result of the introduction of sin into God's perfect creation. God may not inflict a tragic event into a person's life, but the nature of this fallen world may be allowed to run its course.

God is more powerful than any of our circumstances.

The most classic book of Scripture to help us understand this concept is the book of Job. In Job's story, we learn that Satan came into God's presence. God called attention to Job's blameless and upright life. Satan replied to God by saying that Job was only faithful because he had it so good. Satan asserted that if Job experienced loss, then he would not remain faithful. God then released Satan to bring calamities to Job and his family that caused the death of all of his children and the loss of all his possessions.

Although in the end Job challenged God, he never lost faith in God, and the Lord restored all of his wealth and much more.

The lesson that we learn from all of this is that our infinite God's reasons for allowing tragedy and loss to affect our lives through disasters are too vast for our finite minds to comprehend. There is no way for us to understand the reason for loss by divine allowance, but knowing why is not necessary for us to find healing and move on.

Inherited Loss

Let's look more closely at losses that come as the result of someone else's mistake or sin, loss experienced through no fault of our own, for which we nevertheless face consequences.

Not all loss is the result of personal failure. In some cases, it is not even within your control. This is what we will refer to as "inherited loss." Inherited losses are things that we lose as the result of the actions of our parents or the actions of other people. These are not changes that have occurred by our choice, but they are losses that all of us may have to deal with at one time or another in our lives.

Let's first examine God's role in inherited loss. Like natural disasters, inherited loss and why it happens is a very difficult subject. I also believe that we may never understand in this life why people are allowed to make choices that hurt others. What we do know is this: God gave man the gift of free will at the time of creation. As a result of that gift, man chose to rebel against God and thus sin entered the world. The consequence of this fallen state is that people may still choose to act selfishly and will often do so at the expense of other people. The most extreme examples of this are seen every time we read the news and see the list of violent events and crimes that go on in our world. But many other examples involving the cruelty of people to each other that we don't read about are lived out every day.

> There is no way for us to understand the reason for loss by divine allowance, but knowing why is not necessary for us to find healing and move on.

While we may not understand why any given incident had to happen, we can be certain that God has not lost control. His promise in Romans 8:28 stands true: "He will work good in all things...."

The "Why?" may not be answered, but the question "What can God do with this?" can be. Part of the process of healing comes from the recognition that God will use this incident or circumstance to establish His purpose in your life. And we find hope in the fact that how God heals you from inherited loss shapes your ability to help others with their problems.

So what does inherited loss look like?

The Story of a Little Girl

Like many examples we use from our lives, it begins with a story. When I used to recite this story, it seemed to fall off my tongue without feeling. I could rehearse this in the most stoic position and had done so without the blinking of an eye, yet I know that it is at the root of some of my deepest emotions. I now understand that my past struggles have helped shape who I am today.

My father, a skilled pilot in the U.S. Air Force, was shot down over Papua New Guinea. Apparently, he was captured by a territorial and aggressive tribal people. His parachute landed in a thicket of trees and a branch impaled his forearm and held him in the trees. After being freed from the tree, he was taken into captivity where he had to use his wits to survive. A clever magician, he wowed the crowd with tricks to gain leverage with the natives. Eventually, in the process of negotiations for his life, he sold the souls of his unborn children to the chief witch doctor and council. Whether you believe there could be such a price or fulfillment of such an agreement or not, the agreement itself and the story thereafter made an impact on what or who was valuable.

As a reminder of the event, he carried a twisted scar on his forearm from the branch that hung him up in the tree. He also carried the scars in his memory of the parachute that carried him off target and of the souls he carelessly sold. Whether psychologically or spiritually, his choice carried him off another target: his bargain with the witch doctor resulted in a heritage of loss. Those lives he bartered away carried the scars from his choice for the rest of their lives.

Growing up in middle America, I was privileged in opportunity and in material things. Backgrounds of Catholic and Baptist religious traditions made way for the compromise of an Episcopalian upbringing. Mix this with patriotism and cocktails, and we were probably a fairly typical American household.

Our family also had a more-than-typical interest in the paranormal. At most of our infrequent family gatherings, we ended up talking about ghosts and weird happenings. The conversations went late into the night, until the act of falling asleep was a scary consideration. Interest in the supernatural realm was a heritage from generations before and carried down to impact current family experiences. Poltergeists were considered distant but welcomed relatives. Kinetic activity in the home became the unsettling, if not pesky, normal.

I believe that God's hand was over me as a child. There is no other way to explain that kind of protection. I experienced many losses and witnessed many horrible things. I shudder to think of the things I'm not even aware of that were prevented from harming me.

I can pinpoint a shift that occurred in my life and the new direction it took. In the summer before all things would change in the physical and hormonal world, there was an ordinary inquiry about God. I was invited to a Christian summer camp where we learned many Bible stories and recited Scripture verses. One particular night, away from the other kids in bunk beds, away from the scheduled events, three or four of us were huddled up in the room of our camp counselor. We wanted to know who God really was "today." We had lots of questions and talked late into the night.

Then the camp counselor asked, "What would you do if Jesus Himself walked in the room?" I had never thought about that, but when I did, I was so completely humbled at the thought that I didn't think I could look up from my already-kneeling position. It was as if the Lord Himself entered our cabin. That night I vowed to follow God's Son. Nothing visibly changed at that point, but I believe there was a seal that would prove to protect and armor my heart in the years to come.

What was done in spirit would not be clearly discerned for years. Yet, the spiritual world was not silent, not dormant. Upon my return from camp, life seemed to carry on as usual. There was no support, no growth, and no development spiritually. Eventually, other things that occupied my spiritual hunger grew stronger and more pervasive. My spiritual hunger was fed with things that were readily available, things modeled by family: ESP practice, séances, astral traveling, transcendental meditation, witchcraft, Buddhism, Hinduism, and mind control.

My father's early death left my mother in the throes of alcoholism in her inability to cope with sudden loss and the new burden of responsibility. Barely a teen, I was faced with circumstances that neither parent would have wished for any of their children. Gone were the house rules; autonomy was based on guesses and survival skills. It wasn't long before my mother's alcoholism turned into a raging drug addiction. I watched as our home was taken over and eventually destroyed by thieves and addicts.

My young life was spent cleaning up the chaos. I repeatedly bailed my mother out of jail and messy and dangerous situations. There were hospital emergency room trips, halfway houses, and the memorable, drug-induced Four-point Baker Act trip to a psych ward. Beyond my mother, there were numerous people that came through our house and brought their sick behavior with them. Ugly, disgusting, and unmentionable things occurred in the house, including human and animal abuse.

For fear of becoming victim to physical and sexual abuse and perversions – not to mention the need to escape the disturbing shock of watching my mother lose herself to drugs and be carried away by various atrocities to the edge of death – I moved out of our home at an early age (the youngest went with another sibling). I kept my finger on the pulse of the goings on with attempts to watch over her. She didn't die the many times she could have or should have, but managed for many, many years to hang on to the outskirts of what life could offer.

Loyalty has a way of setting you apart.

Every member of our family was affected, and for two decades the constant upheaval shook the tenuous ground we walked on. What was left of our family unit was now separated and struggled to find various ways to survive. Darkness had overtaken our world. There were four murders in our family line during this time. What retirement plan my father had was now ruined, our inheritance squandered away.

For me personally, there was no one to set up boundaries that teenagers need. There was no one to model effective coping skills, no reinforcement of proper social skills. Academics were left to the mood. There was no one to identify my personal attributes, recognize milestone accomplishments, or point me in a purposeful direction toward competence and success. Failure in these important developmental areas magnified my feelings of inferiority, multiplied my unsafe behaviors, and reinforced patterns and belief systems based on lies.

I found myself in a twisted mess, with custody of the youngest sibling in the family, all before I was 17 years old. I became care-manager for my mother – financially and emotionally – until the end of her days. I don't recall thinking much about long-term goals or a personal career. Most of my energy was spent on immediate survival and the caretaker role I inherited.

This was my (inherited) lost first.

Inherited Loss in the Bible

A good Biblical example of someone who experienced a first loss that was not of her own doing is Ruth. Ruth's story takes place in the Promised Land after Joshua had led them in and conquered the territory. It occurs before the time of the Kings, when the people were led by judges raised up by God to overcome challenges to the freedom and safety of His people.

Ruth is a story of wandering, of loyalty, and of despair. It is a story of inherited loss, but most of all it is a story of triumph for those who put their trust in the Lord. The story begins by introducing us to the family of Elimelech, his wife Naomi, and two sons, Mahlon and Chilion. A famine in Israel drove Elimelech and his family to a place called Moab. The Moabites are descendants of Lot's eldest daughter (who had an incestuous relationship with her father). The Moabites were also known to worship a false god named Chemosh.

The Moabites and Israelites hated one another. Because Elimelech and Naomi were devout Jews, it is thought that it was the severity of the famine that drove them to Moab. It was here that the inherited loss began.

Jews were specifically forbidden to intermarry with non-Jews. The decision was made to go and live among the Moabites. As a result, his two sons married Moabite women: Orpah and Ruth. Both sons later died, leaving all three women widows.

Naomi's circumstances were the result of the famine (outside of her control) and the choice to live in Moab (a choice that she and her husband made). Orpah and Ruth both inherited the loss of their husbands. This was further complicated by the interracial nature of their relationship and the choices Elimelech and Naomi made.

When Naomi learned that the famine had lifted in Israel, she decided to return home. The three women started out together, but Naomi realized how difficult it would be for her daughters-in-law to enter a foreign land. There was not even the assurance of any near relative to take care of Naomi, let alone the women she was bringing with her. So she released Ruth and Orpah to go back to their own country and families. For Orpah, the difficulty was too much and she accepted Naomi's offer. She wept, kissed her mother-in-law goodbye, and returned home. Nothing more is said about Orpah.

Ruth, however, was determined to follow Naomi, and her loyalty to her mother-in-law and devotion to Yahweh is what sets her apart as a model for overcoming inherited loss. Her plea is a model of loyalty and the catalyst for God to bring about healing and victory beyond her inherited loss:

> "But Ruth replied, 'Don't urge me to leave you or to turn back from you. Where you go I will go, and where you stay I will stay. Your people will be my people and your God my God. Where you die I will die, and there I will be buried. May the Lord deal with me, be it ever so severely, if even death separates you and me.'" (Ruth 1:16, 17)

After returning to Bethlehem, Ruth agreed to help support Naomi and went to the fields to glean what the harvesters left behind. Boaz was a close relative of Naomi on her husband's side and a wealthy land owner. Boaz is called a "Goel." The term refers to a relative who comes to the rescue and involves redemption. Known also as a *Kinsman Redeemer*, a "Goel" could avenge the blood of a murderer; he could also buy or sell family land and revive the family lineage. Boaz saw Ruth gleaning after the harvesters and took special interest in her.

At Naomi's instruction, Ruth went to Boaz and lay down at his feet at night. This was in essence a proposal from Ruth to Boaz. Boaz was an older man and was touched by Ruth's affection toward him. Boaz was not the closest relative and had to clear their marriage first with the closest relative (who did not want to risk his family's inheritance with another woman). So, Boaz and Ruth married and had a son named Obed, who is the father of Jesse and David, who eventually became king. Ruth was David's great-grandmother and a direct ancestor of Jesus.

Lessons from the Story of Ruth

The story of Ruth can help us understand how to deal with inherited "Lost Firsts." Let's identify the losses that occurred.

First, they lost their homeland. A famine drove Naomi, her husband, and their two boys to the land of Moab. This wasn't a choice to move for a change of scenery or to follow a job prospect. It was a necessity for survival. The repercussions are exponential. This family lost their homeland, family and friends, support structure, and church. Their connections with community weren't just about friendship. People depended upon those relationships to barter for food and other daily needs. Their interaction was necessary to obtain medicine, equipment, and tools. Midwifery was part of the network ... the list goes on and on.

> Loyalty is the evidence of a belief that there is something or someone greater than our problems – a life beyond our loss.

Even today, it is possible to lose your traditions, your culture and mores, even language. One modern-day example might be the tragedy that occurred to the people in New Orleans after Hurricane Katrina wiped out their homes and neighborhoods, and they were forced to relocate.

For Ruth, the next inherited loss was the loss of Elimelech, Naomi's husband. He was the provider for the family and the one who gave them a voice in the community. Life became significantly more difficult without a male leader of the family to provide for them and forge a future for the family. Naomi lost not only her provider but her mate and best friend. Her boys lost their father.

Naomi still had her two sons. At least with male offspring, there was some hope, as they could work to help provide for the family.

The third loss was their spiritual compromise. As devout Jews, they had been warned against living in close association with Gentiles and idol worshippers. Intermarriage was expressly forbidden for Israelites due to the danger of importing false religion into their faith. In this case, the spiritual compromise was that Naomi's sons married Moabite women.

Physical weariness and mental fatigue can naturally result in moral wandering as strength to resist temptation is reduced. When necessity moves us physically, we must stand staunchly against spiritual laxity.

The last loss was the death of Naomi's sons. Why the sons died is somewhat inconsequential. The fact is they died, leaving Ruth and her sister-in-law without husbands, financial support, or offspring. Moving with Naomi to the land of her people left Ruth without even her homeland.

How Ruth faced and overcame her inherited loss is where we find hope and guidance for facing our losses. The key to overcoming may be found in understanding the true cost of inherited loss. When we look past face value and examine the consequence of loss, then the door to understanding and moving through inherited loss opens.

The Value of Loyalty

At the heart of Ruth's victory over her inherited loss was the choice to be loyal. I believe that this is a critical step when it comes to our healing and victory as well. Loyalty is the evidence of a belief that there is something or someone greater than our problems – a life beyond our loss. To embrace this kind of loyalty, we must be willing to accept two critical character traits: the willingness to be submissive and the courage to be bold.

The importance of submission was attested to by Ruth on three accounts: Naomi, her mother-in-law; Boaz, her kinsmen redeemer and ultimately her husband; and most importantly, Yahweh, the God to whom she chose to commit. Through Ruth's willingness to submit, she left the door open to be conformed to God's Plan.

Pride or fear can be extremely detrimental to healing from any loss, but especially a loss that we have inherited. To protect against the insecurities or cope with the strong emotions that come with inherited loss, we may develop a thick skin. But the very coping mechanism that protects us against insensitivity or insult can keep us from being open to instruction or opportunities and block our ability to recover.

God's call for us to trust Him and forgive others is frequently counterintuitive to our survival instincts. For that reason, we will often resist the very acts of submission that enable God's future plans for us to unfold. We must understand that submission is a choice, but to make that choice we must be able to learn to trust again. The key to trusting is, of course, finding someone who is trustworthy. Though men may fail you, God will not, even if we are not faithful to Him.

> "…God is faithful, who has called you into fellowship with his Son, Jesus Christ our Lord." (1 Corinthians 1:9)

> "…if we are faithless, he remains faithful, for he cannot disown himself." (2 Timothy 2:13)

Additionally, loyalty often requires boldness on our part. It involves being willing to leave your comfort zone. It is hard enough to leave our comfort zones in trivial things, let alone the larger, more impactful areas of our life. In order to sense God's peace and fulfill our calling and purpose in life, we must be willing to move through the doors God opens for us. For people who do not like change –

which includes most of us – this may be a particularly difficult thing to do.

Boldness does not always mean acting. There will be times when the Lord calls us to "*stand firm*" when fear or pride screams at us to "run!" or "do something!"

> "Moses answered the people. 'Do not be afraid. Stand firm and you will see the deliverance the Lord will bring you today....'" (Exodus 14:13)

> "Stand firm, and you will win life." (Luke 21:19)

We need to remember that there are seasons in our life. There is a time to run and a time to stand still and know that He is God. I recall part of a teaching on seasons of life that I heard a very long time ago: "...there are times we are to cast our nets into the sea, there are times when we are to draw the net in as a harvest and there are times to sit on the beach and repair our nets...." The willingness to listen to and obey His voice is utmost to the fulfillment of His promises and call on your life, and it frequently requires great boldness.

Loyalty to an idea or person beyond our problem is key to healing, but it is important that our loyalty is not blind, misguided or misplaced. The value of loyalty in times of trouble is found in the object of your loyalty, why you choose to be loyal, and how you express your loyalty. It is good to evaluate and prioritize these things. Are we more loyal to our job than to our marriage? Or to our fraternity or friends than to our church? We need to clearly define our priorities.

God's call for us to trust Him and forgive others is frequently counterintuitive to our survival instincts.

One of the most noteworthy things we learn from Ruth's journey was her loyalty, not only to Naomi, but most importantly to Yahweh. She said:

"…Your people will be my people and your God my God."
(Ruth 1:16)

Ruth's choice to make Yahweh her God was not simply a matter of convenience. Without the intermarriage, Ruth may never have known who the God of Israel was. In ignorance, she may have continued to serve the god of Moab. Even if she had questioned her beliefs regarding the god Chemosh, there may have been no way to come to know the Lord God in her native culture. When she married into a Jewish family, she was exposed to the truth of who God really is. It was then that she made a choice as to whom she would follow.

It was not out of convenience or personal ambition that she chose to stay with Naomi. This path, for all practical purposes and by all appearances, was a dead-end road to a failed future. But Ruth saw something that Orpah, her sister-in-law, failed to see. She saw that the God of Israel was more powerful than her circumstances and that loyalty to Yahweh and His people would result in a future of victory over her losses.

The Difference Between God's Plan & God's Purpose

To understand how we can overcome an inherited loss we must understand the role that God plays and the difference between His WILL and His PURPOSE. I became keenly aware of this while overcoming my own inherited loss. Two scriptures were particularly helpful:

> "In their hearts humans plan their course, but the Lord establishes their steps." (Proverbs 16:9)

> "Many are the plans in a person's heart, but it is the Lord's purpose that prevails." (Proverbs 19:21)

Proverbs 19:21 looked similar to 16:9 when I first read it, but as I meditated on this passage I realized it was different. It went deeper! This passage burned in me an image of God's providence and faithfulness. Yes, man does plan what he is going to do, but God will prevail. What makes this passage even more powerful, especially in the face of failing marriages, major unemployment, lack of morality, etc., is what this passage does not say. It does not say that God's "will" prevails, but that His *purpose* prevails. There is a difference between God's will and His purpose.

Man can thwart God's *WILL* because of the free choice that God has given us, but we cannot block or hinder God's *PURPOSE*. This theme runs throughout all Scripture and history. Adam's sin opposed God's will but did not change God's plan. The rebellion of the Israelites and later the Jews contradicted God's will, but it did not derail God's purpose. This is further evidenced by Christ's guidance in the Lord's Prayer to include a petition regarding God's will. "...*Thy will be done, on earth as it is in heaven.*" This is testimony to the fact that, while God's will is kept perfectly in heaven, the same is not the case on earth.

At the cross we find will and purpose together. As Christ hung between two convicted criminals, fulfilling God's purpose of restoring mankind to Himself, the men on either side of Christ were allowed to exercise their free will. Their choice was to believe or not to believe in Christ. One thief (along with the Pharisees) taunted Jesus to save himself and the three of them. The other thief chided the first and, in repentance and contrition, asked Christ to remember him. The latter received forgiveness and was accepted by Christ.

People have the ability to – and frequently do – undermine God's will. Submitting to God's perfect will requires an active effort, and it can be undermined by others around us. Joshua and Caleb were open to the will of God to march into Canaan, but the fear and stubbornness of the rest of the Israelites superseded them and God. Nonetheless, the purpose of God was fulfilled and Israel did ultimately take ownership of the land at a later time. God illustrated the power of His purpose as He spoke to His prophet Isaiah:

"...so is my word that goes out from my mouth: It will not return to me empty, but will accomplish what I desire and achieve the purpose for which I sent it." (Isaiah 55:11)

Even the great evangelist, St. Paul, warred against the will of God as Saul, but he did not block God's purpose. Instead, he was drawn right into the center of it. The radical change of direction and incredible effectiveness of Paul's life leave little doubt in my mind that Paul had in mind Proverbs 19:21 when God inspired him to write to the church at Rome. (Interestingly, of the 42 references to the word translated "purpose" in the Bible, 19 are from Paul.)

Romans 8:28, "...and we know that in all things God works for the good of those who love him, who have been called according to his purpose," is a perfect bookend to Proverbs 19:21, "Many are the plans in a person's heart, but it is the Lord's purpose that prevails." The hope of God working good in all things is based upon the unshakable promise that the Lord's purpose will prevail.

There is a great sense of freedom and hope that comes from this realization. I have long prayed for God's will to be done, as I should, but I have also become distressed by the willful disobedience and the disregard for God's will and the consequences for doing this. My greatest concern is not only for the disobedient, but for the others who are hurt by their disobedience. This passage brought that all back into perspective. My plans or anyone's plans may fill our hearts, but whether we are well-intentioned but misguided or in open rebellion, these plans will not alter, diminish, or destroy God's purpose. That is a promise from God and therefore has a 100% guarantee. This is wonderful application of the Sword of the Spirit to counter the temptation to give in to frustration or despair.

Isn't it wonderful to know that we live in His grace, not a hyper-grace that continues to live in the freedom to sin without repentance, not one that goes about life flippantly, but a grace that accepts us where we are, forgives us for our sins, and allows us to move forward in life under His direction? He is a God of second chances. He is a God of multiple chances.

Another analogy that comes to mind is that of a portable GPS. This incredible technological device is able to detect its exact location within a couple of feet and then determine the best path to get to a destination that the driver programs into it. What is interesting is what happens when you do not follow its directions. As soon as you deviate from the course, the voice on the GPS announces, "Recalculating." It then proceeds to give you new directions based upon your new location. If it feels that you are going in a direction from which there is no alternate route, it will direct you. "At the next intersection, make a legal U-turn…" No matter where you go or how often you ignore the directions, the GPS keeps calculating until it gets you where you need to go.

> We cannot waste precious energy and time worrying about things that won't change and can't be corrected.

So it is with God. His purpose is sovereign. It will prevail. But since His will for us is subject to our stubbornness, He is constantly "recalculating" the pathway to His purpose. Because of His omniscience, God does not actually "recalculate" because He already knows and has planned for our disobedience. The ultimate correction was on the cross. But the beauty is that no matter how many times we make a wrong turn, God is still able to get us where we need to go. There is no place we can go that God is not able to fulfill His purpose in us. Furthermore, even acts of rebellion and indifference by others that thwart God's perfect will in our lives are not enough to block or hinder God's purpose for us.

In Acts 2, Jesus promises us the Holy Spirit to guide and direct us. God put in our hearts a desire, a bent toward, and an affection for things that bring fulfillment. On the other hand, our enemy – our flesh, the world, Satan – also put in our hearts an attraction to things that can and will destroy us. That is why seeking God daily and being daily directed by His Holy Spirit is of the utmost importance. He will not contradict His Word. So knowing what His Word says is most helpful to our pilgrimage on this earth. And although our flesh, our sinful nature, our misguided approach to life at times, and even our disobedience distracts us, His purpose, in plan A or plan B or plan C, will ultimately reign, as we submit to Him.

What Can I NOT Do About My Inherited Loss?

Knowing what we cannot do about our loss is very important so that we don't waste precious energy and time worrying about things that won't change and can't be corrected. It is critical that we realize that things that can't change don't need to change in order for us to move forward. We don't need a new past to make for a bright future. As a matter fact, it may very well be that the only way to fulfill God's purpose for us is that we have the experience of our inherited loss. So, what is it that we cannot control about our inherited loss?

We can't control our past or future. That is a reality. But it is not what happens to us that matters, but rather how we respond to it. Nevertheless, for us to respond in a favorable way we must first come to understand a vital concept:

What happened to you does not define who you are.

We are not the product of our circumstances, though we will be defined by how we react to them. Our character is defined by the attributes we exhibit when we face adversity. Our circumstances have very little to do with even defining our character. They are simply a showcase in which we demonstrate who we are. The problem comes when we assign more power and authority to our circumstances than they are due.

It is also worth noting that we are not defined by what we are capable of doing, but rather what we actually do. All of us are capable of overcoming any loss we have faced, whether inherited or of our own doing. To accept any other belief is to be completely without hope and doomed to live as a puppet. It is also important to note that the ability to overcome loss is not found in our own strength, but rather the strength that God gives us. He alone is our certain victory in every aspect of our lives. That said, not everyone takes advantage of God's strength and exercises their ability to overcome. To the degree that you choose not to use God's power to overcome, you define yourself and your character by what you do *not* do. The world and the devil may define you as a "loser." God defines you as a "winner."

> "…for everyone born of God overcomes the world. This is the victory that has overcome the world, even our faith. Who is it that overcomes the world? Only the one who believes that Jesus is the Son of God." (I John 5:4-5)

The question now is how you define yourself.

The world can try to define us. Our parents can try to define us. Our school or clubs can try to define us. Our peer group can try to define us. But God is the only One who can truly define who we are, for He created us. Scripture tells us He knitted us in the womb and He knew us before we were born. He designed us each uniquely for His plans and purposes. He has good things in store for us. He is the One from whom we should get the definition of our uniqueness. He sees our heart and doesn't judge us on our appearance or our past or things to come. God's definition is not based on our actions or our lack thereof, not on our successes or failures. It is based upon who He created us to be. It is based on our great value to Him, which is attested to by the blood of Christ.

We cannot control what has already happened. We can allow Him to edit our past and change our future by changing our present.

> "…Not that I have already obtained all this, or have already arrived at my goal, but I press on to take hold of that for which Christ Jesus took hold of me. Brothers and sisters, I do not consider myself yet to have taken hold of it. But one thing I do: Forgetting what is behind and straining toward what is ahead, I press on toward the goal to win the prize for which God has called me heavenward in Christ Jesus." (Philippians 3:12-14)

What happened to us (spiritually, emotionally, and to some degree physically) does not limit what God can do with us in the future. It is so easy to believe that we are "damaged goods" and play the role of a victim. We start to look at all of our wounds and we see them as limitations or handicaps. We evaluate the quality of life by all of the things that we can't do because of the things that have happened to us in the past. We begin to look at ourselves as disabled and use that as an excuse for not doing what we could do or even trying to do what we are called to do.

We aren't handicapped; we are simply different. People with physical differences have long found ways to compensate for their differences. Blind people often have heightened senses of hearing, touch, and smell. Many people have limitations, yet they are able to compensate by excelling in other areas.

Some go so far as to celebrate their uniqueness. I came across one of the most excellent examples of this while taking a class on sign language at a school for the deaf and hard of hearing. I learned a lot about what they refer to as the "deaf culture." The deaf culture is a lifestyle. The deaf have embraced their uniqueness, and a beautiful, expressive language was born as the result of it. They consider themselves to be a people group in much the same way others look at ethnicity. I became most aware of how passionate they feel when someone asked the instructor if he would get cochlear implants to gain the ability to hear. His answer was an adamant "no." He went on to say that most deaf adults would answer the same. When asked why, his response was even more fascinating. He said that there was nothing wrong with deaf people and they did not want to give up the uniqueness of their culture any more than a Caucasian, Hispanic, African American, Asian, or Native American wants to give up their heritage.

> What happened to you does not define who you are.

In the same way, our best chance to overcome our inherited loss is to embrace the person that we are because of it. It takes more than just determination. We must also feel secure and accepted. Like the "deaf culture" we need an "inherited loss" culture. We find that in Christ Jesus and in a personal relationship with Him. He not only accepts us but He also uses our past as a catalyst for His power to be released in us.

> "Concerning this thing I pleaded with the Lord three times that it might depart from me. And He said to me, 'My grace is sufficient for you, for My strength is made perfect in weakness.' Therefore most gladly I will rather boast in my infirmities, that the power of Christ may rest upon me. Therefore I take pleasure in infirmities, in reproaches, in needs, in persecutions, in distresses, for Christ's sake. For when I am weak, then I am strong." (2 Corinthians 12:8-10 NKJV)

His strength is made perfect in our weakness. God is the provider of our power and success. Those who have suffered loss may be in a unique position to receive God's power. It is not just the need for a particular experience that empowers us to be more available; the humility that comes from our past can make us more susceptible to God's power.

As long as you believe that you can handle a situation, that you are self-sufficient, you will not seek help. Once you recognize your failure and weakness, you'll be able to yield to God and truly become the best you can be. If you want to fulfill a God-sized purpose, you will need to have God-sized power. This can only come through humbly admitting your inability to accomplish the task and yielding to God's ability to accomplish what you cannot.

What I CAN Do About My Inherited Loss

We may not have had a choice in what happened to us earlier in life, but we do have a choice every day about how we live our lives now. We may have been hurt very deeply by our inherited loss, but it is not an excuse to treat others harshly. We simply do not have to continue bad behavior. We can make the choice to live differently. Just because we lived with alcoholic parents or an alcoholic spouse doesn't mean that we must become an alcoholic ourselves. Because our parents neglected us doesn't mean that we must also neglect our kids. We can choose to act differently.

It starts with taking our thoughts captive.

> "We demolish arguments and every pretension that sets itself up against the knowledge of God, and we take captive every thought to make it obedient to Christ." (2 Corinthians 10:5)

> "Our thoughts open the door to actions; therefore, it is essential that we take our thoughts captive. But each one is tempted when by his own evil desires he is lured away and enticed. Then after desire has conceived, it gives birth to sin; and when sin is fully grown, it gives birth to death." (James 1:14-15 Berean Study Bible)

We may not always be able to avoid unwanted or destructive thoughts and memories from entering our minds, but we most certainly can control what thoughts we accept or dwell on. While we cannot simply decide not to think negative thoughts about our inherited loss, the key is to displace those negative thoughts with positive ones.

> "Finally, brothers and sisters, whatever is true, whatever is noble, whatever is right, whatever is pure, whatever is lovely, whatever is admirable – if anything is excellent or praiseworthy – think about such things." (Philippians 4:8)

The more you take your thoughts captive, the easier you'll find it becomes to make better choices regarding your actions. This process would be difficult or impossible in most cases to do on your own, but you do not have to tackle it without help. Christ has given us His Holy Spirit, and a part of the character of the Spirit is self-control. Through the presence of the Spirit in you, it is now well within your power to take captive your thoughts and replace them with godly thoughts.

We can also control our willingness to forgive. Although we will be discussing the role of forgiveness throughout the book, it's important to state first of all that forgiveness is a choice, and we can be in control of it. We must be careful of harboring resentment toward those who hurt us. The irony of harboring resentment is that it seldom hurts the perpetrator and almost always hurts the victim. Thus, it actually doubles the hurt and damage to the one who has been given an inherited loss. Not only is there no peace, but the resentment robs you of your time, as well. We are keeping ourselves prisoners when we don't forgive. We are the ones that are held in bondage while our perpetrators walk free. Forgiveness does not mean whoever hurt us was justified; it does not mean we condone what they did; it releases them to God's hand and allows Him to deal with the person and their actions. Our willingness to truly forgive brings with it peace and freedom. Forgiveness is essentially setting down a heavy weight.

> We may not always be able to avoid unwanted or destructive thoughts and memories from entering our minds, but we most certainly can control what thoughts we accept or dwell on.

One practice in our family is that, after a trip to the grocery store, we try to make as few trips as possible to get the groceries out of the car and into the house. It is not uncommon of each of us to carry as many as 10 grocery bags at a time. Carrying all of those bags quadruples our diameter and makes it very difficult to open doors or even go through them. The sheer weight makes it almost impossible to raise your arms or shoulders and you cannot carry them far. There is no better feeling than when you get to the kitchen and can finally set them down. Sometimes they weigh so much that we just set the bags on the floor because we cannot lift them to counter height. The funny thing is that it stings for the first moment after you let the bags go as the blood rushes back to your fingers and as the strain on your arms and shoulders subsides. Then the relief is wonderful. You even sense that your arms are lighter than they were before you lifted the bags.

In the same way, forgiveness brings relief from the incredible weight of resentment. Moreover, resentment breeds more resentment and soon we find that our emotional arms are maxed out, carrying bag after bag of resentment. It may feel awkward to lay this down as you may have become used to the weight, but it will change very quickly to joy as you experience the freedom and relief of living without the weight of unforgiveness.

> "But to you who are listening I say: Love your enemies, do good to those who hate you, bless those who curse you, pray for those who mistreat you. If someone slaps you on one cheek, turn to them the other also. If someone takes your coat, do not withhold your shirt from them. Give to everyone who asks you, and if anyone takes what belongs to you, do not demand it back. Do to others as you would have them do to you." (Luke 6:27-31)

> "Whatever you have learned and received and heard from me, and seen in me, put these things into practice. And the God of peace will be with you." (Philippians 4:9)

Another area that must be brought under control is our attitudes. Attitude is not just what you think about; it is your disposition based on what you do with those thoughts, how you lay them alongside your experience – in short, your perspective on life. You can choose to live with a positive attitude about your future and act with confidence.

You can also choose not to live like a victim, in an attitude of self-pity. It may be tempting to remain a victim when you've been hurt by others. But you are called to forgive those who have hurt you.

In Matthew (18:21-22), the apostle Peter asked Jesus how many times we are supposed to forgive. Jesus said "up to seventy times seven," an amount most scholars agree was meant to imply infinity. A cartoon on Facebook not long ago showed the disciples trying to do the math on the Scripture reference. The caption read: *It is easier to forgive than to do the math.* Funny as it seems, if we don't forgive, we cannot move on.

Believe in yourself and what God can do through you. Remember your value to God: He sent His Son to pay the price for all our sins and allow us a restored relationship with God and ultimately eternal life. You can affix the crown He put on your head, adjust your cape, and win the world through Christ with the knowledge of how He values you.

Refuse to let your past define you. Take your thoughts captive. Forgive. Remember your value to God. These choices can play a pivotal role in healing from an inherited loss and your ability to successfully move on. They are positive choices that can change your current status and shape the success of your future. But none of them are possible without the help of God through the power of His Holy Spirit. With His Holy Spirit, there is nothing that you cannot do.

> "I can do all this through him who gives me strength."
> (Philippians 4:13)

Preparing to Re-Engage

In order to re-engage, to move into the future God has purposed for us, we must intentionally participate in life, rather than simply allowing it to happen to us.

How do you prepare yourself to re-engage? First of all, allow time for healing from your inherited loss. But understand that time alone is not the issue, and the clock does not start ticking until you recognize that you have inherited a loss first and you begin to come to terms with the loss. If you re-engage too soon, you risk repeating history. Take time to sit under solid Biblical teaching; soak in times of worship. Be willing to sit on the beach and repair your fishing nets before casting out prematurely. Be an observer of Christ's life; be an observer of your life. Glean from others' mistakes; glean from your mistakes. Get counseling, if necessary, to see objectively the places you may be working out of guilt, out of hatred, out of unforgiveness, out of wanting to prove or please someone rather than truly serving God alone.

Don't be afraid to break up fallow ground, to let go of the hardened layers you have developed to protect and defend yourself.

> "Sow with a view to righteousness, reap in accordance with kindness; break up your fallow ground, for it is time to seek the Lord until He comes and rains righteousness on you." (Hosea 10:12 NASB)

It is so easy to harden our hearts to protect ourselves after we have been hurt. The challenge is in letting go of the desire for self-protection. The fear is that we will be vulnerable and defenseless if we allow others to come into our lives and get past our defense mechanisms. The reality is that, if we yield to God, we are not defenseless. God is our defender! It doesn't mean that people will not be able to hurt us, but simply that we find acceptance by God more essential than acceptance by people.

Be willing to see things from a different perspective and do things differently than you have before.

Forgive those who may have been responsible for your inherited loss. Let go of the anger and resentment for the hurt you received. More than being "willing" or "knowing that I can choose," you must forgive; otherwise, everything we have discussed is just an intellectual exercise. This may be very hard to do, but you will never achieve the fullness of what God has in store for you if you harbor unforgiveness.

What makes forgiveness harder yet is the popular misconception that, if we forgive someone, we have "let them off the hook." The truth is that, even though we forgive them, they still are accountable for their actions – just not to you. Their accountability is to God, and He will judge them based upon how they respond to His Spirit's work with them.

Additionally, there is the mistaken belief that you must meet, face to face, the person who caused your first loss. Not only is this not the case, it may not be possible if that person has passed away, or may not be safe if they are abusive. The most important step in forgiveness is being true to yourself and to God. Commit to forgive them and let go of the resentment that the offense caused. You have much to gain.

> "For if you forgive other people when they sin against you, your heavenly Father will also forgive you. But if you do not forgive others their sins, your Father will not forgive your sins." (Matthew 6:14-15)

Lastly, be teachable. Be willing to see things from a different perspective and do things differently than you have before. Set aside your pride and seek the help of godly people, especially those who have faced similar losses. As God prompts you to change and others give you godly counsel, you must be willing to act on that prompting and counsel. Though humans naturally resist or even fear change, the truth is that change has already occurred when our inherited loss was initiated. The challenge you now face is being open and willing to complete the change and come full circle to the place where God's purpose is fulfilled, and what the enemy intended for bad can be used by God for good.

Additional Discussion Questions

- Have you experienced an inherited loss?
- Are there things you are holding on to?
- Do you need to forgive someone?
- Is there anything else that is preventing you from moving on?

Prayer to Heal From an Inherited Loss

Heavenly Father, I ask you to help reveal any losses that I may have been given through circumstances or the actions of other people. Strengthen me to let go of the hurts that I am holding on to; enable me to see the effects of this loss, and help me, by Your Holy Spirit, to overcome the effects of this loss in my life. Help me to forgive those who have caused this issue in my life and guide me to see myself, not by the loss, but in light of Your love. In Jesus' name, Amen.

CHAPTER THREE

FORGIVENESS & GRACE

In the last chapter, we began talking about the role and importance of forgiveness in dealing with a lost first. We have spoken about the importance of forgiving others who may have been responsible for causing your first loss. But this is just one piece of the puzzle of forgiveness. As a matter of fact, it would be difficult, if not impossible, to forgive others if we do not do two other things first: We must seek and accept the forgiveness of God through Christ Jesus for any part we may have played in our loss; then we must be willing to forgive ourselves.

At the root of forgiveness is the concept of grace. The literal definition of grace is "undeserved love," but there is an acronym that describes it better: God's Riches At Christ's Expense.

God is the one constant in an otherwise constantly changing world. As the creator of the world and specifically our Creator, He is the only one able to grant us unquestionable forgiveness and restoration. Grace is not the result of God simply dismissing our sin and ignoring His own rules. It comes to us by way of a sacrifice made on our behalf to pay for those sins, through the life, death, and resurrection of Jesus Christ. To understand grace, we must first understand God's love for us.

> "For God so loved the world that he gave his one and only Son, that whoever believes in him shall not perish but have eternal life. For God did not send his Son into the world to

condemn the world, but to save the world through him."
(John 3:16-17 NIV)

In this chapter, we will examine God's love for us and how it manifests itself in GRACE. We will also look at God's role in grace and forgiveness, as well as ours. We will seek to better understand the role of healing and how it opens the door to new opportunities.

Ah, Grace!

In the last chapter, I (Jerri) told of my home life and how my mother slid from a seat of elegance to the banks of debauchery. I do not speak of these things to defame my mother or blame her. I am not to judge her and point fingers at her. I am reminded of the adage attributed to John Bradford (1510-1555) who said, "There, but for the grace of God, go I."

Although I believe I endured critical losses because of addictions that my mother succumbed to, there are also memories that are precious and dear to me. I see in myself and in my children some things that are a testimony to who she was. To deny them would be an injustice to her character and life. She was a most beautiful woman with a gracious and giving heart. She had an enviable wit and the gift of making people feel valued, especially the elderly. She was a very generous and thoughtful woman. Her love for animals is one of the attributes of our family today.

The sophisticated wife of a prominent Air Force colonel, my mother knew how to play the part of wife and hostess well. I regret that I was not able to learn more about who she was. I know that she was in nursing school when she married my father and followed him overseas. I knew snippets of her childhood. Her mother, too, was a nurse – and a divorced woman at a time when that was taboo. I heard stories of how my mother and her sister had to stay in an orphanage while their mother worked in a tuberculosis sanatorium, and how they were bullied and mistreated there.

My mother suffered many losses in her own life that surely affected how she related to life. I always felt her love for me was ambivalent. When I became a Christian, some of my deepest burdens were for her. I prayed for her for years and years. I wanted to see her in heaven one day. I'm sure I was able to forgive her and love her and pray for her because of God's own love for me and how His grace affected my own life. I'm equally certain that I did not follow the path she chose for this same reason – although there was a time in my life, long after becoming a Christian, when I was fragile and in despair could have given in to the temptation to turn down such a path.

I am happy to say that my years of concerned prayer were answered. She did discover God's saving grace before she died. She prayed and gave the last bit of her life to Him. One afternoon when I went to visit her, I knew she was at death's door. I was able to say my final goodbye. I held her hand and squeezed it three times, our family code for saying "I love you." I did not anticipate a response as she was no longer lucid, so I was dumbfounded when

> Allowing us to live out our choice is an act of love, as we are given the room to learn the futility of our ways, so that we might appreciate the grace that is always available with our Father.

she returned the code and shocked by her sudden acute awareness of the moment. It was as if a veil between the living and those who had gone on had been pulled aside and I was witness to a holy place. I began to cry. She asked why I was crying, and I told her how difficult it was to say goodbye. She agreed and told me of her regret that she would not be able to see her grandchildren grow up. She looked away, caught between two worlds – the physical world where I sat beside her and the spiritual world that I was not privy to. She then described what she saw. With a look of peace and anticipation, my mother saw her firstborn; he had been murdered in his young adulthood, some years before. I thought at that moment she would jump out of her body. She was saying she had to go and bidding me farewell. She then said she saw the Lord, and it was at that point that I pressed her to tell me his name, as she had served many "lords." She answered that his name was Jesus, God's Son. She looked at me and told me she was "going home."

And there it was: grace. Ah, grace! There is grace when we fall short. There is grace that brings us home. There is grace to welcome us back into the fold. There is grace to come home to. We must be gracious in our dealings with people, for they are like us, and – with shaking knees I state – we are like them.

Lessons from the Prodigal Son

In Luke 15:11-32, Jesus tells a parable to describe God's grace. Most of us have heard the parable of the prodigal son, but if you are unfamiliar with the story, you will enjoy the read. For the sake of this lesson, I will summarize it here:

The story is of a father who has two sons. The younger son became impatient with his life and demanded his inheritance which the father gave to him. He left home and squandered his money on wild living until he was broke. In desperation, he resorted to the lowest job imaginable, feeding pigs. During this time, he came to his senses and realized that his father took better care of his servants. He decided to ask his father for a job as a servant.

When he was some distance from home, his father spotted him and ran to greet him. Instead of condemning him or treating him as a servant, the father embraced him and reinstated him to his position as a son. He then announced the son's reinstatement and the joy of the father through a feast.

The parable of the lost son is one of the most powerful explanations of what the grace of God is and how much God loves us. While whole books have been written about this parable, I would like to focus on four key points that Christ makes in this story.

First of all, because He loves us, God will give us the freedom to move away from Him. I know it may sound strange that a loving father would allow a child to act disrespectfully and then leave, but love gives us a choice. We do not have to stay with God, and we also do not have to leave. What Jesus is saying is that the choice is ours to make.

In the parable, the youngest son decides that he no longer wishes to stay home under his father's authority and provision. His perception of the world was that there was more fun to be had in the world than at home. So he calls upon his father to give him his inheritance and then leaves to pursue the indulgence of his flesh. What may be overlooked in the English interpretation of this parable is the grave implication of the son's request and departure.

In the Hebrew tradition, a son's right to his share of the inheritance was receivable only upon the death of the father. What the son was actually saying was that his father was dead to him and he had no further use for him. He was simply an obstacle to the son and his pursuit of pleasure. It was not just that he wanted to leave; he was burning his bridges behind him. What is most fascinating in this parable is that the father took the son's insults and consented to his son's wishes, even though he knew that it would lead to ruin. The father did not have to do this. He was not obligated to give the son anything and was well within his right to disown the son for his rebellion. Moreover, he neither begged the son to stay nor did he follow the son to bring him back.

This is a testament to the love that our Heavenly Father has for us. He is not obligated to put up with our sin and rebellion and well within His rights to curse us for our insolence toward Him. It is also within His ability to forcibly bind us to His will so that we have no choice but to obey Him. Nevertheless, our Father, out of perfect love, gives us the freedom to choose against Him and the room to live out our choice. And what is most amazing is that He doesn't stop loving us when we do. That is not to say there won't be consequences for our rebellion, but even in the consequences God's love never fails. Allowing us to live out our choice is an act of love, as we are given the room to learn the futility of our ways, so that we might appreciate the grace that is always available with our Father.

The second point is that, after the prodigal son "came to his senses," he did not assume he had a second chance with his father. He went back to the farm, hoping to be a servant. Even with all that he knew about his father, the son still made no assumption that his father would take him back as anything more than a servant. He wasn't even positive that his father would accept him as a servant; he was practicing his appeal along the way home. In a day and age of "entitlement," it is important to note that God's grace is not owed to us. The very fact that it is not owed makes it grace – undeserved love.

You can become your own worst enemy when you refuse to forgive yourself for the failures you have committed.

The third point is that we can know that God will always receive us back. While the son may not have had any expectations of the father welcoming him back, it was apparent that the father had not stopped yearning for his lost son. Though the father did not run after his son to bring him back, he never took his eyes off of the road, but watched to see if he would come back. Not only was he waiting, but when the father saw his son coming back, he didn't wait with a stern I-told-you-so look on his face. Jesus tells us that the father ran to meet his son before anyone else could get to him.

In the Jewish culture of that day it would have been considered very undignified for an older man to run and even more so for an insulted father to run and embrace the rebellious child who had insulted him. Moreover, it would have been the responsibility of the servants to remove the rebellious child from the property by force. This father forsook dignity. Out of love and for the sake of the safety of his son, he ran to get to him before anyone else could.

He then put a ring on his finger, a symbol of restored status in the family. In the same way, our Heavenly Father never gives up hope for our return. He anxiously awaits the first sign of our return so that He can run to meet us. Upon any indication of our contrition, God is there to rush to us and bring us back into His arms and restore our status as His son or daughter.

The last point is that God restores the lost with joy and thanksgiving. The parable tells us that once the father had received his son back, he called everyone together and hosted a party to celebrate. Jesus tells us in Scriptures:

> "I tell you that in the same way there will be more rejoicing in heaven over one sinner who repents than over ninety-nine righteous persons who do not need to repent." (Luke 15:7)

Only two times in all of the Gospels is there a reference to "angels rejoicing." The first was at the birth of Christ and the second was when a lost sinner repented and was brought back into the family.

Lessons from the Woman Caught in Adultery

In addition to the parable of the lost son, there is an incident in Jesus' ministry that has given us a real-life example of God's grace at work. The incident was actually the result of the Jewish religious leaders trying to trap Jesus and discredit His ministry. The fact that the accusers were less interested in moral purity and spiritual faithfulness than they were in defaming Jesus is evidenced by the fact that they only brought the woman who was caught in the act of adultery and not her male partner. Again, there are whole books dedicated to all of the lessons to be learned from this story, but we will focus on three of the most important.

> "The scribes and the Pharisees brought a woman caught in adultery, and having set her in the center of the court, they said to Him, 'Teacher, this woman has been caught in adultery, in the very act. Now in the Law Moses commanded us to stone such women; what then do You say?' They were saying this, testing Him, so that they might have grounds for accusing Him. But Jesus stooped down and with His finger wrote on the ground. But when they persisted in asking Him, He straightened up, and said to them, 'He who is without sin among you, let him be the first to throw a stone at her.' Again He stooped down and

wrote on the ground. When they heard it, they began to go out one by one, beginning with the older ones, and He was left alone, and the woman, where she was, in the center of the court. Straightening up, Jesus said to her, 'Woman, where are they? Did no one condemn you?' She said, 'No one, Lord.' And Jesus said, 'I do not condemn you, either. Go. From now on sin no more.'" (John 8:3-11)

The first key lesson is *"...all have sinned and fall short of the glory of God"* (Romans 3:23). When the Pharisees brought the woman before Jesus, they thought that they could trap Him by using the sin of an individual as a litmus test of Jesus' spiritual wisdom and faithfulness. What Jesus did in reply is a reminder to us all. So often we seek to elevate ourselves by highlighting the failures of others, or we allow the judgments of others to define us. What we learn here is that no one can elevate himself because of the sin of others, nor should anyone denigrate himself due to the sin that he has committed.

There was not a person present there who was without sin, except Christ Himself because He is God (neither is there on the earth today). Jesus challenged the Pharisees with the concept that if they did not choose to extend grace, then their authority to carry out judgment must be sinlessness. Note that He did not say "the most righteous" can cast the first stone. Righteousness was subjective in their eyes. They all thought themselves righteous. But sinlessness is objective, and none of them could claim it. The observation that the oldest ones recognized their unworthiness first is fascinating. It wasn't until the younger ones saw the conviction of their elders that they began to listen honestly to their own consciences.

Secondly, it is noteworthy that Jesus did not condemn the woman after everyone else had left. When humble sinners come to the Lord for help, He is always faithful in His healing grace.

It is even noteworthy that Jesus did not choose to "accuse" the Pharisees of their sin either, but rather let their consciences convict them. When challenged with sinlessness, it was their inner knowledge of their own conduct that caused them to drop their stones and walk away.

Only the enemy condemns us. Condemnation is for the purpose of oppressing or crushing us. Conviction gives us the opportunity to respond and receive GRACE. This is why Jesus convicted the Pharisees and will convict us when we stray. He desires that all have the second chances we need, and Jesus was willing to die to make certain that we would have those second chances.

The third point is also integral. Forgiveness brings a change of lifestyle. Jesus said to the woman, "Go and leave your life of sin." Grace is free, but it is not cheap. Grace cost Jesus His life and He asks for ours in response to His sacrifice. Not that we have to physically die, but that we "die to sin" and "die to our old sinful lifestyle." The true evidence of God's grace having been effective in someone's life is found in the fruit of change. A changed life yearns to be more Christ-like and adhere to the Law. This is not to achieve righteousness, but because by grace we have Christ's righteousness in us. We strive to be more faithful and obedient out of gratitude for the grace we have been given. We turn away from the sins of lust and greed, sexual sin and envy, selfishness and malice, pride and arrogance. The more that grace takes root in our lives, the more it will be evident to all around us by our actions and attitudes. It is not that we never sin again, but our life's goal is to strive for sinlessness by the power of God's Spirit. We lean on Christ's grace for the times we fall short.

Grace Overcomes Entitlement

As I stated earlier, Scripture indicates that God does not owe us a second chance. As a matter of fact, not everyone gets a second chance. There are those unfortunate incidents where someone tries a drug just ONE time and dies from an overdose, or when a drunk driver is killed in a car accident. I have witnessed other people who were recklessly living out their second chances after a divorce by living promiscuously and died before they changed their lifestyle. The common denominator to the lost second chance is death.

The analogy I like to use to help people understand this is the stock market. When a person buys into the stock market they, on paper, own a part of that company and its profits and losses. The value of that stock, on paper, goes up or down based upon the value of the company. But it is all on paper. You have no more or less money in your bank account with the changes in the stock value. The only time the change is realized and becomes permanent is when the stock is actually sold.

It is not that we never sin again, but our life's goal is to strive for sinlessness by the power of God's Spirit. We lean on Christ's grace for the times we fall short.

In a similar way, when we are born we have stock in both our temporal and eternal existence. Because of God's gift of free will, we have the ability to choose to increase our eternal value or decrease it. By God's grace He gives all of us chances to increase our eternal value by faith in God through Christ Jesus. Most are given many chances, but the chances are not limitless. In the same way that selling the stock makes the value of the stock permanent, death makes our choices with regard to our eternal existence permanent. The biggest difference between the two is that you cannot control the value of stocks, but you can choose when to sell. In life, you choose to increase or decrease the eternal value of your life, but you don't choose when you die and make it permanent.

So why do I tell you this? It is a reminder that you should not assume you will have many chances and use that assumption as justification for making bad choices now. You need to make choices every day that would be good if they were the last choices you ever made.

When we fail, we must come to God with a heart of humility and He will give us cause for confidence. Look at his promises to the humble as opposed to the entitled:

"A bruised reed he will not break, and a smoldering wick he will not snuff out. In faithfulness he will bring forth justice." (Isaiah 42:3)

"My sacrifice, O God, is a broken spirit; a broken and contrite heart you, God, will not despise." (Psalm 51:17)

"But God demonstrates his own love for us in this: While we were still sinners, Christ died for us." (Romans 5:8)

"But he gives us more grace. That is why Scripture says: 'God opposes the proud but shows favor to the humble.'" (James 4:6)

It is also essential to approach second chances with a thankful heart. Cherish the opportunity that some are not given. Remember, a second chance is not a reflection of failure, but an opportunity. It is, as it were, a dessert, when your main course is the temptation of bitterness or failure of the first loss. Focus ahead. Look up. Look to The One who can redirect, rearrange, reestablish, and redeem.

How wonderful to be able to create something new – a new job, a new place to live, a new reputation, etc. We have already acknowledged that change can be difficult. We all know that there are repercussions to bad choices in life. Sometimes consequence leaves us with limitations, and we must adjust to a new normal. Sometimes we lose everything and must begin all over, recreate ourselves. It can be painful until we once again sense purpose in our lives.

But if we remember that second chances are opportunities, we will be able to approach them with thanksgiving. If we understand that these second chances are a gift of God's grace, we can avoid the pitfall of entitlement.

Many first losses may actually be blessings in disguise. There are times that you may be better off because you no longer have what you once had or no longer "are" who you used to be.

Receiving Forgiveness from God

For us to truly live in God's grace we must first accept the foundation of forgiveness. No second opportunity can truly succeed unless we embrace the gift of forgiveness. The fascinating thing about forgiveness is that, in its essence, it is extremely simple, as its origins are from God. At the same time, forgiveness is also very complex in its application to our lives and our circumstances. By this I mean that forgiveness comes from God and is not earned. We do not have to "find a way" to make it happen. However, we must desire it and ask for it. We must understand ourselves enough to know that we need it. We must humble ourselves to accept it. And we need to understand the difference between contrition and self-abasement in preparing to receive the gift. On our own, this would be impossible, but a part of God's grace is the discernment and ability to receive that grace.

> A second chance is not a reflection of failure, but an opportunity.

We have already spoken about the need to forgive others for the hurts that they caused us, but the only way this is truly possible is that we have first received forgiveness ourselves. You cannot give what you do not have. Our forgiveness of others will come out of the overflow of the grace that exists in our lives. Therefore, there are two levels of forgiveness that we must seek and embrace. First you must seek and accept forgiveness from God. Then you must be willing to forgive yourself. Only when both of these have occurred will you be able to forgive others, if necessary, and move forward.

The question then arises: Have you received forgiveness from God for the "lost first?"

> "If we claim to be without sin, we deceive ourselves and the truth is not in us. If we confess our sins, he is faithful and just and will forgive us our sins and purify us from all unrighteousness." (1 John 1:8-9)

Our need for forgiveness may be self-evident, and God's promise to forgive unshakable, but the question here is, "Are you willing to receive God's forgiveness?" That is not something that can be assumed.

Consider the difference between Peter and Judas. Both Peter and Judas betrayed Jesus the day before He was crucified. Judas reported Jesus' location to the religious leaders for money, and Peter denied he knew Jesus after swearing he would stand by Him. Both men were forgivable, but only Peter was forgiven in the end. Why? Because, even though both men knew the severity of their sin and both men were deeply sorry for their sin, only one believed that God was able to forgive him. Peter remembered the warning of Jesus; he repented and knew he could be forgiven. Judas never really had a relationship with Jesus as Savior and saw no hope. He was so filled with remorse and hopelessness that he not only rejected God's grace, but he made his choice permanent by committing suicide.

How can we avoid the mistake of Judas and receive the grace that Peter experienced? Let's go back to the directive of 1 John 1:8:

> "If we claim to be without sin, we deceive ourselves and the truth is not in us."

To claim that we are without sin is to deceive ourselves. Your part in the "lost first" is to acknowledge and confess your sin. You must take ownership and responsibility for your part. It is easier to close the door when all the skeletons have been removed. Anything left unresolved and unforgiven is ammunition for the devil to use against us in the future. These are things that will keep coming up again, and again, and again. They must be forgiven to be forgotten. That is not to say that we have to fabricate a false humility and make up a sin so that we have something to confess. There are more ways to sin in a first loss than simply to have caused it.

Think about Job. Even his friends kept accusing him of having sinned and causing his losses, but the Lord testified that Job did not sin in this way. Nevertheless, by the end of the story, Job did have to confess the sin of challenging God's divine justice and fairness.

As a result of his submission and confession, God not only forgave him but also restored many times more than Job had lost.

So, what areas do you need to examine to determine what you need to lay down before the cross?

Actions are the first area that you need to examine. Did you in any way sin in your first loss through your actions morally, ethically, or spiritually? If you were at fault, it is important to remember that there is no sin too great to be forgiven.

Next, have you sinned by your attitude? It is possible to do the right thing, but do it for the wrong reason. If the wrong reason is itself a sin, then you must lay that before the cross or risk continuing to be condemned for it by the devil.

We need to seek forgiveness, not only for the things that we have done, but also for the things we didn't do – but should have.

> "If anyone, then, knows the good they ought to do and doesn't do it, it is sin for them." (James. 4:17)

It isn't just about doing the wrong thing; we have a responsibility to do the right thing. So often our biggest offenses are found in the area of our inactivity or our justification of our inactivity. Frequently, pride will protect this area of our lives more than it defends the sins we commit. Know this: if we do not admit this failure and seek forgiveness for it, the enemy will use it against us again and again in the future.

We need to seek forgiveness for harboring resentment, contempt, or unforgiveness while we were victims. But just so we don't end up with either unresolved or, in some cases, unnecessary guilt, let us make a clear distinction here: resentment and anger are not the same thing. So often, people regard anger as sinful. Anger, in and of itself, is not wrong. We will and should be angry at injustice and cruelty, as God Himself is. But that is where we must draw the line. We cannot withhold forgiveness or harbor resentment toward others as a result of the harm they may have caused us.

It is up to God to deal with the sins of others. We will never find satisfaction by giving into resentment, contempt, or unforgiveness. As a matter of fact, just the opposite most often occurs. We end up feeling guiltier sometimes than the people who caused us the first loss to begin with.

Trust God to forgive you for the sake of Jesus Christ. We are only a prayer away from having the sins of our past wiped away, leaving a clean slate.

> "'Come now, and let us reason together,' saith the Lord. 'Though your sins be as scarlet, they shall be as white as snow; though they be red like crimson, they shall be as wool.'" (Isaiah 1:18 KJV)

We must learn to take Jesus at His word. Remember God's promise in 1 John 1:9: "...*if we confess our sins, God is faithful and just and will forgive us our sins and cleanse us from all unrighteousness.*" That is God's promise, and He does not go back on His word. The only thing that can separate us from the love of God is our own unwillingness to accept that He can and will forgive those who repent. This was the difference between Peter and Judas.

Even the ability to believe is a gift from God, empowered by His Holy Spirit. If you are struggling to believe that you can be forgiven, ask God for help and He will give it to you – even if you have never had a relationship with Him before!

A Renewed Spirit

The change that comes as a part of God's grace comes by God's hand and not your own. This is so important. We will always struggle with the ability to be a different person by our own power, but it is God who brings about change in our lives, including the ability to ask for forgiveness.

He is the One who empowers us when we simply accept Him and yield to His Spirit. Therefore, ask God to give you a renewed spirit.

What does it mean to be given a new spirit or to be given a renewed spirit by God? It means there will be faith where only doubt existed. It means there will be understanding where there once was ignorance. With this new spirit, we are able to see ourselves the way God sees us, and we can view past events in light of how they can move us forward in our God-given purpose. It is more than just understanding that we are forgiven, but that we are positioned perfectly for God to fulfill His purpose in us. It means that we stop believing the lies that we are unforgivable or defined by our failures. It means that we can change the recording that the enemy would love to keep playing in our minds.

In order to move forward, we must put an end to any words from our past or present that berate us, words that defined us outside of how God defines us. We must be careful about what we believe about ourselves. How? By seeing ourselves the way God sees us. By His Spirit, we are able to understand the truths about God's relationship with us and our relationship with Him.

It would do you well to heed Isaiah and put a watch-guard at the door of your mind, blocking the negative thoughts of your past:

> "Forget the former things; do not dwell on the past." (Isaiah 43:18)

Then you must change your focus.

> "Finally, brothers and sisters, whatever is true, whatever is noble, whatever is right, whatever is pure, whatever is lovely, whatever is admirable – if anything is excellent or praiseworthy – think about such things." (Philippians 4:8)

The key is that you do not simply decide to stop seeing negative things, but that you displace them with the truth of God's Word as revealed by His Spirit. You must change the well from which you drink. You will always have memories of your past. It is natural to focus on all of the pain and failure of the loss, but the Holy Spirit will enable you to *edit or recompose* your memory, to see your past from a different perspective.

Many times we cannot move forward because we are replaying our failures or sufferings over and over. We can also replay our vengeance or imagine how we would redo our circumstances – when God clearly wants us to move on. There may never be an opportunity to go back, but we can have the Lord come into our memories and show us His role in what happened to us, so that we can be healed and move on.

Editing, for this purpose, is to take something hidden in the darkness and bring it in to the light, allowing the light to expose the truth and permit a different, possibly more objective perspective. When we see the color white with our eyes, it is actually a blend of all the colors, while black is the absence of color. I was taught that, in photography, the opposite is true. In photography, white is the absence of color and black is the blending of all colors. Photographers can pull apart areas of black on a photograph and draw out various colors and images, making something – that was not previously seen – visible.

The process of *recomposure* is similar; it is allowing God to reveal Himself in your past and bring to light truths that will set you free. God is always present. The truth that He reveals will undeniably tear down the false beliefs you have about yourself. If you perhaps believe you are of no value, based on a parent or teacher's reaction, you will learn that you are a highly valued creation – regardless of how someone failed to show it. The Lord can show us what we may not have seen in a past situation – especially if it was seen through the eyes of a child.

You have the opportunity to allow God to enter into your memory and show you His unshakable love for you. God can enter into your hurting or vulnerable places and show you His fingerprints – the evidence of His love, grace, forgiveness, and mercy will promote healing for the broken places in your life. This is retrospective healing, editing with anecdotal vision. The process is hindsight; you revisit your circumstances, but this time you can see GOD's provision.

Learning to Forgive Yourself

The other piece of living in God's grace is learning to forgive yourself. So, have you forgiven yourself? It can only be accomplished by first experiencing forgiveness from God. This is so critical because the Bible teaches us that the enemy stands ready to accuse and condemn (Revelation 12:10 & John 10:10). No matter what we believe about God's forgiveness, the enemy will use our self-abasement to condemn us of the same sin over and over and over again.

You can become your own worst enemy when you refuse to forgive yourself for the failures you have committed.

There is a story about a man who had a dream. In this dream, the Lord asked him to turn over all of the keys of his life. While most keys he gladly and willingly handed over to the Lord, there was one key that he tried to hold back. He thought he could hide it and the Lord would not notice. The key locked a room he was very ashamed of. The room contained a history of all of the darkest secrets and most disturbing actions of his life, and it was overstuffed from all of the years of throwing things in and slamming the door before it could all fall out. But the Lord knew of the key and of the room, and He again asked the man to hand him ALL of the keys.

> Cleaning up after your first loss may not be painless, but don't mistake these consequences for God's punishment or disapproval.

Reluctantly, the man handed over the key to the room of secrets. Once He had the key, the Lord immediately walked to the door to open it. The man closed his eyes and cringed with fear at the revelation of all of his sins and failures, for he was certain it would all come crashing out. To his amazement, there was no sound at all. He opened his eyes, only to find that the closet was empty.

"I don't understand," said the man. "What happened to everything inside?"

The Lord replied, "It has been empty since the day I died to free you from them. It was only your belief that the room was full that held you hostage to it."

As we have said, in order to forgive yourself, you must accept the forgiveness of Christ Jesus. To do that, you must learn the difference between *condemnation* and *conviction*.

Condemnation does not come from God; it is the work of the enemy who is seeking to rob us of hope. The sad truth is that our own sinful nature is more than willing to aid and abet the enemy in selling us out. Then, once we lose hope, we become easy prey.

Though we are guilty, God chooses not to condemn. Instead, the Lord will convict or make us aware of our sin, but always with the goal of forgiveness and restoration. His desire is to bring us freedom from guilt and shame. He wants to give us hope so that we can be sure of our victory and future.

What to Do with the Grace You Have

With God's grace comes a changed attitude. With His grace comes a changed lifestyle. There will be a willingness to forgive as we have been forgiven.

The gift of forgiveness and grace doesn't mean that there won't be temporal consequences. There may be victims of your "lost first." You may have legal responsibilities and/or financial consequences as a result of your choices or actions. Issues of trustworthiness or confidence may have to be overcome with people you have hurt.

Cleaning up after your first loss may not be painless, but don't mistake these consequences for God's punishment or disapproval. Although you must pay consequences, it does not mean that God's purposes are thwarted. He may restore what was lost as you head down a different path than before. He may bless you with even better success in the second chance than you gave up in the first. Whatever you face, God will help you make the most of your experience to fulfill His purpose for your life.

Lastly, be careful not to gamble and forsake your current situation because of difficulties or challenges you face. If you have been given another chance at something, do not be hasty in throwing it away, anticipating that a better chance will come along. Every opportunity comes with challenges. Remember, we are not entitled to grace or guaranteed a second chance. We need to live every day and take advantage of every moment to maximize what we have been given and, by God's grace, we will succeed!

Are you ready for a second chance?

For Discussion/Reflection:
- What am I going to do with the grace given to me?
- How will I live differently?
- How will I be different?

Prayer to identify your loss
Heavenly Father, thank You for the grace You have given me, though I have done nothing to deserve it. I thank You for Your unconditional love that sacrificed Your own Son to save me from sin. Help me to forgive others as You have forgiven me and to forgive myself, because You have declared me forgiven. I pray that you will enable me to live in that grace every day. In Jesus' name, Amen.

CHAPTER FOUR

THE OPEN DOOR

In the first two chapters, we addressed the concept and impact of first losses. In the last chapter, we looked at grace, with an overview of healing. We noted that healing may take time and you need not be in a rush to seek out second chances. As a matter of fact, there is a real danger in rushing into a new opportunity before you have healed sufficiently. Once you have healed, a part of the freedom that God gives is a new opportunity. You can turn your sights toward the future. We can open the door to a second chance.

Door #1 ... Door #2 ... Door #3?

In the 1960s, before the boom in TV game shows, there was an iconic game show called *Let's Make A Deal*. It was most remembered for the crazy outfits audience members wore in an effort to get selected as contestants. The show's host, Monty Hall, would offer each contestant a choice. The choice would most frequently be a curtain (covering a stage), a large box, or a door. The contestant had to guess which one contained the prize. What complicated it more was that there was typically a "good" prize in one, a "great" prize in another, and a "zonk" prize in the third. If that wasn't challenging enough, once contestants made their choices, before the prize was revealed, the host would often offer cash for their choice.

Once their choice was made, the prize they had given up was shown first, and then their actual choice was revealed. Prizes ranged from cars to new appliances to a mule as a zonk prize.

The show still runs today, although with a different host. The interesting thing is that people often make their choice based upon the size or appearance of the option. And while a curtain is big enough to hold a car, sometimes curtains open to reveal a zonk, while the small box may contain keys to a brand-new car hidden offstage.

Second chances are frequently like that. We are not confronted with *a* door, but rather multiple doors, and curtains, and boxes. The challenge is not just determining which choice is a "good" one, but which is the "best" option. As with the game show, appearances can be deceiving. The difference is that life is not a game show. Our choices may impact us and others for the rest of our days. There is a real danger in trying to make that decision based upon appearances.

To make the right decision we must first understand what a second chance is and what it is not. Then we must learn to decide when an open door is an OPEN door.

It is possible to confuse our will for God's intent when we see a new opportunity. The danger is that many of us want to quickly rectify or fix our lives after we recover from an initial crisis. Most of us do not like the incubator period. I know I don't. I sometimes forget or want to skip the period of healing.

I (Jerri) learned a lesson about patience in healing through a personal injury when I tore the rotator cuff in my shoulder. As much as I wanted to go back to the gym after my injury and resume my weight training regimen, I was unable to do more than simply move the arm itself. The rotation of the shoulder alone was painful. It was quite some time before even a 2-pound weight could be lifted without pain and repercussion. Too much weight or movement of my shoulder caused a setback and the need for re-healing.

Many months were devoted to waiting. There was nothing visible, but inside, over time, slight changes occurred. Gradually I was able to lift heavier and heavier weights. It took over a year to regain most of my range of motion. To this day (a couple years later) I do not have the full mobility I had prior to the injury.

Likewise, in an effort to get our lives back on track, we try to move ahead in life at our previous pace, sometimes moving ahead of our wounded self – sometimes moving ahead of God.

Abraham's Choice

Consider the story of Abraham. As we learn in Genesis, Abram (as he was originally known) was living in the land of Ur in the Chaldeans when he was called by God to leave that place and go to a land that the Lord would give to him as an inheritance. Abram did not know where he was going when he left his country, his friends, and his family to follow God's call. In response to Abram's faith, God made a covenant with him, that his descendants would be as numerous as the stars, and that they would inherit the land of Canaan. The Lord would be their God, and they would be His people. As a sign of that promise, God renamed him *Abraham*, which means "Father of Many."

> The tough challenge we face is that human logic and reasoning often present themselves as God-given opportunities.

There was just one problem. Abraham did not have any children, let alone any sons. And his wife, Sarah, was evidently infertile. And he was getting older – much older. As he assessed the situation, he was faced with a choice. God had given him a door, the door of faith that God would fulfill His promise in His time and His way. But that was not the only door he saw. He saw a door of opportunity to handle things his way. If Sarah was infertile, then maybe he could have a surrogate in Hagar, Sarah's handmaiden. So with Sarah's consent, and even encouragement (Sarah would need sons to care for her in her old age, after her husband was gone), Abraham slept with Hagar and had a child by her. The son was named Ishmael.

Although God eventually gave Abraham and Sarah another chance through the gift of a son, Isaac, even in their old age, the effect of the first loss was enormous. What seemed like a good choice at the time proved to be a disaster that affects the entire world to this very day.

So, what can we learn from the life of Abraham about open doors?

Don't Impose Your Plan on God's Purpose

The first lesson from Abraham's story is not to take matters into your own hands. There is seldom a time when you have only one choice. Abraham did not have just one choice. What's more, his choice was not to simply trust God or not trust God. Satan will not always place a clearly bad choice in the mix. The choices we face are not always black and white. Abraham's choices were: a) continue by faith to believe that God would work in some unknown and incomprehensible way to provide a child through Sarah, or b) use human logic and reasoning to achieve what seemed like a practical solution to the problem. Simply stated, the choices were to have a son through intercourse with Hagar or trust God to handle it His way.

The tough challenge we face is that human logic and reasoning often present themselves as God-given opportunities. Furthermore, we may start to question whether we really heard from God correctly the first time. Just remember that "Did God really say...?" was Satan's question to Eve in the garden. The heart of the matter is knowing that the path we are on is one God has called us to.

All of us are called. Abraham was called to go to Canaan and be the father of a nation. Your call may be much simpler: to repent, to be a husband or wife, or to be a parent. Your call may be to a secular career with witnessing opportunities or to manage your finances in a more godly way. Don't sell your call short or neglect the promises that God makes regarding His help and empowerment to fulfill that call. God made a promise to Abraham, and God continues to make promises to us – promises He will keep.

Seek the guidance that God will provide and resist the urge to take matters into your own hands.

Have Patience – "Not Now" Is a Real Answer

Despite Abraham's faith in God's promise to him, he acted out of impatience. Being patient can be the hardest part of choosing the best door. Abraham was not acting in faith when he made the choice to have a child by Hagar. He bought into the false adage, often quoted as Biblical truth: *"God helps those who help themselves."*

It is not as though he decided God was not going to make good on His promise. In fact, the Bible indicates just the opposite; Abraham is held up as the model of faith. It appears as though he was simply under the impression that God was waiting for him to make the first move. But that got Abraham in big trouble, and it will do the same for us.

Most of us don't have a natural ability to wait well. Impatience can be our greatest challenge in choosing the best door. Here's why: we lack sufficient wisdom to make the first move. Unlike God, we cannot know in advance the outcome of our choices. We are not in the appropriate position to reason out the best course of action. The good news is that God does not expect us to act apart from His guidance.

Knowing when we have received God's answer to our prayer for guidance, though, can be difficult, especially when the answer is "wait." "Yes" and "no" are much easier to understand and be certain of, even if we don't like the answer. We may ask ourselves, "Did I hear from God to wait, or did I miss something?"

When we let a choice pass, and another does not take its place quickly, we question whether we should have acted – or even worse, whether we missed our only chance and lost our opportunity. These thoughts are not divine promptings, but rather the work of the enemy who still tries, as he did in the garden, to get us to believe we have misheard.

The enemy would love nothing better than to make us believe that we missed our opportunity with God, and now He is frustrated with us. The devil wants us to believe that God is waiting in silence for us to act in order to "take advantage of His faithfulness." Our own sinful nature is ready to agree. The truth is, God does not wait in silence for us to act. God not only actively calls us when it's time to move, He will keep calling us if we do not hear it the first time. We don't have to guess or wonder whether we heard or not. By grace, Jesus, who has experienced life as we do, advocates before the Father and gives us His Spirit, not only to call us, but to keep calling us. We do not have to question God's faithfulness.

> Few possess the natural ability to wait well. Be careful that impatience does not take advantage of you!

Samuel, a prophet and the last of the Israelite judges, struggled to understand the call of God to move out when he was just a child. In 1 Samuel, chapter 3, we read of the call of Samuel. Dedicated to the Lord by his mother at birth, Samuel was taken to the temple to work for the high priest, Eli, when he was still a young boy. The Bible tells us that one evening Samuel heard a voice calling his name. He assumed it was Eli and ran to him. Eli dismissed it and told him to go back to bed. This happened a second time and Eli told him the same thing. It was not until the third time that Eli figured out that God was calling the child. Eli told Samuel that the next time he heard the call again, he should reply, "Speak, for your servant is listening." God had a plan for Samuel's life, but Samuel first had to learn to hear God.

God is faithful. He will call us. His grace is evident in His patience with us. If we do not hear clear direction from God on something He has promised us, then the call is to wait. It is important to note that waiting does not necessarily mean that we do nothing.

Waiting is an activity in itself. During this time we are to make the most of where we are and learn all we can. We may be given small opportunities, chances to grow and prepare for the day when God calls us to move forward. We should prayerfully examine our lives during this season to make certain we do not miss God's direction, even as we wait (in faith) for His direction to become clear, knowing the door will open when it is time to move forward.

Part of being vigilant while we wait is to be discerning of other voices. We need to raise a red flag at any voice that calls us to "figure out" what "I" need to do next. When it is time, God will call – and keep calling. Until then, we need to be okay with the fact that "Wait. Not at this time" is a real answer from God.

Don't rationalize/minimize potential ungodly outcomes

When we act on our own, we do so without understanding the potential issues and consequences that will result from that decision. Ishmael's presence became a major issue for Abraham and Sarah when their promised son Isaac was born. Frequently, the efforts we make to take matters into our own hands have unpredictable consequences, things we cannot account for. But sometimes we disregard what we do know.

Abraham and Sarah were not unaware that there would be issues that would arise from Abraham having a child with Hagar, Sarah's handmaid. Jealousy was bound to be an issue. Nevertheless, Sarah consented – more than that, she encouraged Abraham to go forward with the plan. Not only did Sarah become jealous when Hagar had a son, but Hagar became prideful and condescending toward Sarah because she was able to do what Sarah could not. The result was great tension, angst, and hostility within Abraham's household and marriage.

Abraham must have been aware of the potential for this disastrous outcome, but he chose to rationalize and/or minimize the risk. He may have believed that the risks would simply not be a factor, since he was acting to fulfill God's promise. When we choose to act to fulfill God's call for us – apart from His express direction – we will likely find ourselves doing the very same thing. If you have to minimize or dismiss the risk of an ungodly outcome, this should be a red flag that you are moving ahead of God. It's time to re-evaluate the choice you are making.

God will not call us to actions that have a high probability of generating ungodly consequences. While it's true that following God's direction may put you at odds with the world and its values, God's guidance will never put you at odds with His values. You will never have to consider compromising God's morals if He is the one calling you to follow His lead.

Trust God for the Ultimate Best Result

There was no way for Abraham to envision the long-term consequences of his actions. He could not have anticipated the struggle between Isaac (the son promised by God and the father of Israel) and Ishmael (the son of Abraham's efforts and the father of the Arab peoples). Abraham could not have known that his decision would have dire repercussions in the world for millenniums, but the effects are felt to this very day; Isaac's and Ishmael's contempt and hatred for each other not only gave birth to the conflict in the Middle East, but the battle and resulting misery continues to spread throughout the world.

Neither can we comprehend the long-term consequences of our actions. When the possible fallout from our choices is delayed past its ability to affect us, we dismiss it as "someone else's problem." This mindset is most evident in the problems we face in our culture: environmental disasters, economic failures, and moral collapse. All are the result of decisions made generations ago by people who did not seek God or rely upon His wisdom and omniscience to guide them.

What may seem right today can easily become a disaster later. It is only by trusting in God, seeking His wisdom, and waiting for His guidance that we can make decisions that will achieve their purpose both now and in the future. We cannot know the long-term consequences of our actions, so we must rely on the only One who does know them ... God.

Repurposing

When we lose a "first chance" we tend to return to the mental and emotional state we were in at the start of our first chance. The problem is, merely reliving a decision will not ensure a successful second chance. We must look at ourselves to discover what led us to make a decision or choice that was destined to fail.

My decision to marry the first time was based on two things: 1) not wanting to be alone and 2) the need to meet the perceived expectations before entering the ministry full-time – i.e., find a wife. What I failed to see at the time was that I was functioning quite well alone, so there was no need to fear being single. Furthermore, trying to meet the expectations of others is almost a guaranteed failure. The process of healing from my lost first marriage involved going back and becoming confident in who God made me to be, and who I am. I learned to live for a season within safe boundaries while God produced growth. I learned not to make decisions driven by fear or false responsibility.

> While it's true that following God's direction may put you at odds with the world and its values, God's guidance will never put you at odds with His values.

Before we get too far into this, we must understand what a second chance really is. Second chances are new opportunities birthed out of a lost first opportunity. Although the pathway exists because of a lost first, not every second chance is a redo of former circumstances. In many cases, the second chance is a redirection from the old opportunity. The opportunity incorporates new circumstances or new directions: a REPURPOSING of our lives.

What does it mean to repurpose? Repurposing is adapting something for use in a different context or for a different purpose. When my daughter didn't have enough kitchen space, we bought an armoire originally intended for clothing storage, but it made an adorable shabby-chic kitchen piece.

In the context of our discussion, repurposing involves being open to the reality that there may be more than one way to use your life or talents. It involves a willingness to be teachable and to learn from your past, but not merely to avoid making the same mistake. A better, more effective choice may be to do something altogether different with your talent or opportunity.

The example that comes to mind was shared by a math teacher I know. She talked about the fact that, while a computer science degree requires extremely advanced math courses, the computer scientist seldom uses the actual math they have learned. Rather, they use deductive reasoning and logic (required to do the initial math) to solve the complex computer problems. In other words, math is not just about numbers. There are other applications for it.

So also, there is more than one application of our life, skill, and talent than what we have done in the past. Don't be afraid to apply your gifts, skill set, and circumstances to a new idea. God is creative and can turn what we consider failure into a useful tool. This is not about just settling for the second chance. It is about the possibility that you were always meant to be so much more than the person you were, your skills and talents meant for greater things. It could be that the second chance isn't just a byproduct of failure, but rather God's original intent – except that you got in His way the first time around. This may well be your greatest opportunity to become who God has called you to be.

Additionally, we need to understand that, while a second chance may mean going to square one, it doesn't necessarily mean going *backward* to square one. What do I mean by that? If your new opportunity takes a new and fresh direction, it may be sufficient that your starting point is where you are today and you move forward from there.

Past, Present, & Future

To grasp the concept of what a second chance is, or to discover whether we are ready for it, we must be able to see it from three perspectives: our PAST, our PRESENT, and our FUTURE.

Understand your past

To see new opportunities, you must first understand and glean from your past. This is more than reflecting on your failures; it is reflecting on who God made you to be. To understand your past, think about what your values are. There are critical things and incidental things to learn from every job, relationship, or experience you have had. We can learn from our failures and successes alike to help us determine who we are and what we are capable of doing. We are doomed to repeat our history if we do not know who we are and who God is before making major life decisions.

Understanding your past is rooted in understanding yourself and your relationship with God. You may well need to build or rebuild your relationship with God. This is especially true if you think you have failed in the eyes of the Lord – or if you think God has failed you in some way. As part of the healing process, it is most important to find out WHO God is. If you were trying to fill a job position, you would get to "know" job seekers by reading their résumés. You would learn what their strengths and goals are, and although you wouldn't know everything about them, you'd have a deeper understanding of who they are by reviewing what they have written about themselves. In the same way, you can get to know God by reading His Word. From His Word and through the evidence of His actions you begin to see who God really is and how He has impacted your life in the past.

Through learning about God's character, you can understand more about yourself. In His Word, God speaks quite a bit about motivation. Knowing what has driven your past choices and actions will tell you a lot about your vulnerabilities. If you do not deal with motivators such as fear and false responsibility, then even second opportunities will be driven by those same things and destined again to fail. That's why so many of us repeat history. Our emotions and life patterns are being governed by the same unmet needs and influences.

Simply masking or distracting ourselves from the problem is not the solution. The only way we find the solution is to discover what motivated us in the first place.

Embrace your present

With an understanding of your past, you can then embrace your present. Despite past failures and losses, you must accept yourself enough to say, "I am okay with who I am now." As you grasp your great value from God's perspective and know that He wants you to succeed – He has plans for you – you can stop making decisions based on unhealthy emotions or false premises. Gone are the "knee jerk" responses.

Embracing your present means having the ability to be content with who you are and where you are at this time of your life. You can only do this by accepting God's assessment of your worth.

Understanding your past and embracing your present may be costly. For instance, I had to become single for quite a season before I was able to have a second chance. But perhaps my first call was to be single, to go out on the mission field, like I'd dreamed of doing as a young teen. Perhaps I was being given a second chance at my first opportunity: to be single again and fulfill some goals in my life that I couldn't while fulfilling the obligations of a married man.

When my marriage failed, it was a call to be single. Jumping right back into a marriage in order to fill that open position in my life would have been disastrous. Being single allowed for a season of growth and discovery. I had to figure out who I was and develop a relationship with God – one on One. After a season under His direction, I was ready to be reinstated in a marriage covenant, this time out of mutual fulfillment and with God as head.

Embracing your present will allow you to be open to your future.

Welcome your future

The next step is to embrace your present: your potential, your passion, and God's purpose for you. I remember God teaching me: "Do what you are called to do (potential); do what you love to do (passion); and be the person that I have made you to be (purpose)." This is important: your second chance may not look anything like your first.

Your new motivation will lead you to surround yourself with people whose values are similar to yours. As you gain experience and energy from doing what He has gifted you to do, the jobs you find will be jobs that advance you toward His purpose for you.

Succeeding at new opportunities requires us to be flexible, teachable, and confident in God's faithfulness. Surrendering our futures to God means relinquishing control to Him. This is not an easy task. We must first die to self; in many cases, that means previous dreams must die as well.

> When you understand your past, you can embrace your present.

But dreams that are rooted in and motivated by wrong thinking – greed, lust, fear, pride, etc. – need to die. The person who made early career choices motivated by the pursuit of wealth or the desire for power and now faces career and/or moral failure, must be willing to let those dreams die in order to find out what God wants to do with the talents He gave them.

So often, our efforts to create our own futures are motivated by unmet needs. We labor with limited insight and knowledge, making decisions based on what we think will make us happy, with no understanding of where true happiness is found or what it looks like. We operate by clichés: "If it feels good, do it!" or "How much is enough? Just one more!" Only when we are willing to surrender control of our futures can the God of life fulfill dreams that are more beneficial and consistent with His plan for us.

Divine Navigation

The key to a successful future is not human insight or feeling, but Divine Navigation. Open Doors, second or otherwise, are developed through an understanding of God's purpose and plan. Where God desires us to be, He is prepared to lead us.

> "The Lord is my shepherd, I lack nothing. He makes me lie down in green pastures, He leads me beside quiet waters...." (Psalm 23:1-2)

> "...He (God), your Teacher will no longer hide Himself, but your eyes will behold your Teacher. Whether you turn to the right or to the left, your ears will hear a voice behind you, saying, 'This is the way; walk in it.'" (Isaiah 30:20b-21 NASB)

He knows the pathway we must travel. His Word is our map, and He is our navigator and our pilot. So, how do we use divine navigation to determine which door is the best to walk through? We start by addressing the following questions: What is it that God wants me to do? What are my desires and values? What are my boundaries and limitations? How much effort am I willing to put into it and at what cost?

To follow the divine map that leads to our success we must examine how He made us and equipped us. Our life journey is one of discovery and progressive movement. If God has designed me with wings, the pursuit of burrowing and cave dwelling is a mismatch. If God has designed me with the claws of a mole and I can burrow efficiently but I keep trying to fly, I am destined to fail. I have to understand how God made me and for what purpose.

Divine navigation includes perfect vision. God is the one all-knowing Entity. He not only sees our future, but He sees the future of all creation. The decisions that He makes are not just for us, in hopes that it does not negatively affect anyone else; He choreographs all people and all creation to work together. Sometimes His call for us to "wait" is not just about us learning patience, but rather to give time for others to accomplish what they need to do so that "ALL" things can work together for good.... The door swings both ways on this one.

To be sure of our next step we must have some concept of where we want to go. Ideally that vision includes both short-term and long-term goals. When our daily goal begins with living in fellowship with the Lord, we stay on track. This is especially important on those days when that is the only goal of which we are certain. Some days must be lived out hour by hour and seem endless. Keeping the Lord our focus will remind us that He has a plan for us. We can go through our daily activities, trusting that He is moving even when we do not see the slightest of changes, let alone drastic transformation. An important aspect of vision is appreciating the value of the small steps we take each day. Whether it is limited to shopping and running a few errands, or just paying a few bills, when He remains our focus and desire, that is progress.

Other times God makes His goals in our lives very clear, and each step we take brings us visually closer to what He has for us. During this season, it is important to keep track of our bearings and work toward the place where God is calling us.

When I owned a boat, I would go offshore fishing or diving. From a distance, the marker buoys were not visible, so I used binoculars with an integrated compass to find the marker buoy, and then noted the compass reading. When I put the binoculars down, the buoy was still invisible, but I pointed the boat in the noted compass direction. It wasn't until I was very close to the buoy that I could see it with my own eyes; I had to act on the knowledge that the buoy was there in the distance and stay true to the bearing in order to get there.

This sort of patient progress is all the more challenging for people like me who like to see results quickly. It is hard for me to follow the path to something beyond the near future. But I must remember that there is a benefit to each waypoint along the journey God has called me to; I must stay the course.

I am often reminded of my favorite quote from Lewis Carroll's *Alice In Wonderland*:

> Alice came to a fork in the road. "Which road do I take?" she asked.
>
> "Where do you want to go?" responded the Cheshire cat.
>
> "I don't know," Alice answered.
>
> "Then," said the cat, "it doesn't matter."

It is so true. If you do not know where you want to go, then there is no point in worrying much about which way you take. God's guidance helps you to understand that you have a purpose and, moreover, what that purpose is. You cannot know exactly what you will become in advance, but if you know enough about God, you can begin to make decisions consistent with what you know about His will for you.

Not only is divine navigation critical for determining if a door is the "best" opportunity, sometimes it is critical for even determining if the door is an opportunity at all. Some doors are just a distraction. These things we will address at length later.

Characteristics of a Second Chance

One of the greatest concerns most of us have is whether we will recognize a second chance when it comes along. While we will delve into this area more deeply later on in this book, there are a few things that we can address now that might help you.

First, recognize that second chances are not necessarily "redos." It might be assumed that a second chance would simply be the opportunity to do the same thing over. Keep in mind that God may give you a second chance that does not look at all like the circumstance you were in before your loss. There are innumerable reasons why this may not be possible or wise. God may not simply have you "take the same test over again." He may want to get you to the same place eventually, but God has infinite ways to get you there. Be flexible!

Sometimes second chances are very obvious and grand. Our second chances may even exceed our initial goals.

We may have made multiple attempts at a ministry or a project, and each attempt may have had resulted in failure. Maybe we lost more than we invested financially. Maybe we lost something very valuable in the attempt – health, a relationship, a dream we worked hard for, or a great job. We can get so task oriented we fail to remember who we are and Whose we are. Sooner or later, we find that we have reached the proverbial end of our rope.

Then – when you have exhausted your strength, ingenuity, and resources – God takes the opportunity to move in your life. Something bigger than you ever anticipated rises from the ashes of your loss ... right out of the broken pieces ... something grander than you could have ever created. But it can only happen if your relationship with the Lord is the foundation of your purpose.

Some second chances are very subtle or even simple

If you held a position of authority and somehow you have lost that position, it will be difficult to start over from ground level. The more ground you've lost, the more painful the progress can be. Remember that we serve the God who reigns on high. He not only has love and mercy to forgive us, He has the power to reinstate us in His plan for our lives. He paid a dear price for you for a reason. Do not allow circumstances to discourage you.

> "Do not despise these small beginnings." (Zechariah 4:10 NLT)

All second chances are valuable and must be cherished. The place or season following failure or disappointment should be treated kindly. Since we likely do not know how God is going to fasten together the broken pieces into something useful, it is wise to be patient. Hold fast – not to what you had, but to Him.

Frequently, second chances come when we least expect them. I always heard that God was an 11:59 God, meaning that just when we were about to throw in the towel ... or just when we were about to lose hope – the wind turns and we have an answer to our prayer. Never lose hope.

"Hope deferred makes the heart sick." (Proverbs 13:12)

I understand more clearly now that answers seem to come when we change – not when we have finally convinced Him to change. *"For He is the same yesterday, today and forever"* (Hebrews 13:8). God seems to be more interested in our state of heart than in our title, position, or timing. There is truth to the old adage, "a watched pot never boils." The more we seek the second chance, the longer it seems to take for it to come. We can get so busy searching out tomorrow that we miss the opportunity to live today. Lost todays cannot be gained back. Wherever you are on the path, pursue God's business, finding joy in His work for you today.

Second chances come as a result of yielding to God. This truth especially rings true for Jerri and me. Years after our respective divorces, we had each learned to live in the day, to do what we were called to do and what we enjoyed doing. Individually, we sought the Lord and lived out His calling for us. God chose this unsuspecting time to bring us together – not at a bar, church, or singles group, but at a bike shop.

I was being fitted for my bike on a Saturday afternoon, and Jerri had mechanical problems with her bike earlier that day. It was just the right time. In addition to our attraction to each other, because of God's choreography, we already shared an interest in cycling, and we became aware of the fact that we were involved at the same church on different campuses. When we patiently yield to God, we find that He is extraordinarily thorough.

Sometimes what we call a loss is actually God's first opportunity for something different. How many times do we take matters into our own hands, only to find out that either we have made a mess out of something or things didn't turn out according to our expectations?

Our lack of submission, our failure to patiently listen for instructions, may result in circumstances that God never intended for us. It costs us loss or ends in failure because the opportunity was never meant to be ours. We may not be given another chance at what we lost, because we were never supposed to be there in the first place. Why settle for a man-made option when we can have an opportunity designed by God?

> When we patiently yield to God, we find that He is extraordinarily thorough.

The good news is this: God meets us where we cry out for help. And though He does not change our past, He can most certainly move us forward. Most of us learn the hard way, but let this go deep into your heart: Jesus has a plan for your life that includes the details of your heart's desire. He is the author of your dreams and knows how and when to bring them to pass.

Who Is Controlling Your Choices

As with Abraham, we face real temptation to take matters into our own hands. It is often not a consciously prideful desire to do things our way. Sometimes we are motivated by fear that we somehow missed an opportunity in the past and are now running out of time and chances. Unless we can look back and see the unmistakable hand of God on a previous opportunity, we need to be patient and wait. Even when we don't catch the open door the first time, if we keep an open heart toward the Lord, He will keep calling us to the open door. When we don't wait on the Lord, the results are never "best" and seldom are they even "good."

Forcing an opportunity seldom yields the results we desire. Fear and need are strong emotions and, when there is loss in our lives, they can be our default setting. These emotions are the antithesis of patience; they prompt us to move ahead of God. When we move to fill a need without the wisdom of God (who sees the future), we lack the knowledge to weigh the long-term effects it will have on our life, or the effect on other people's lives. That is why it is especially important to draw close to the Lord and allow for His healing plan before we set out to "fix" things.

Anybody reading this book knows the outcome of moving in our own strength. Even when we have a degree of success apart from God's guidance, it does not bring a deep sense of purpose and fulfillment. The only thing that brings true peace is the unmistakable knowledge that we are in the center of God's will and plan for our lives.

Discerning the difference between a second chance and a forced opportunity is a real challenge. It is of utmost importance to routinely be in God's Word, to be in fellowship with Christian accountability partners and/or mentors, and be under the teaching of sound doctrine. When you seek the godly counsel of others, you are most likely to be listening, not to your emotions, but to God, who has a plan for your life.

> "Plans fail without advice, but with many counselors they are confirmed." (Proverbs 15:22 ISV)

Learn to be patient. Let God work. Patience is so difficult when we are aching for something that may be missing from our lives. Patience is easier found when we see God working, when there is evidence of His hand at work. It can be grueling when there is silence or when it seems nothing is going on. The battle is in the mind. Waiting can feel like being left behind. Questions plague us, and doubt and fear can creep in. Remember how God has worked in your life in the past. If you do not have a history with God, then look at the stories in His Word. Understand that you may have a lesson to learn first, but He is faithful. He has not, nor will He ever, forget you!

When you give your future to God, He will work His plan from your starting point – wherever that may be. He has actually been working in your life since before you were born. His work can be unseen, but it is vital. He is moving, weaving, crafting, tilling, planting, watering, and causing growth. By the time a flower blooms, it has already been through the preparation of many seasons. Don't be discouraged. Many things happen in the waiting room. Moreover, we may be spared problems or conflicts by waiting. I have always wondered how many things I have been spared because God was working on my behalf when I wasn't even aware of His presence.

When we trust God with control of our lives, we unleash the full power and potential of what He can do for us. Pastor Steven Furtick said, "If He (God) always met our expectations He would never have the opportunity to EXCEED our expectations." Our view is so limited. The old adage is true: "We don't know what we don't know." How, then, can we count on our own expectations about anything?

On the other hand, God is! He is above and beyond our expectations, exceedingly and abundantly. This is articulated so well in the beautiful prayer that the apostle Paul prays for the Ephesians:

> "...and to know this love that surpasses knowledge – that you may be filled to the measure of all the fullness of God. Now to him who is able to do immeasurably more than all we ask or imagine, according to his power that is at work within us...." (Ephesians 3:19-20)

How can we be patient? Christ's Spirit is the source of our ability to be patient. The Bible teaches in Galatians 5 that the "Fruit of the Spirit" includes patience. That means when the Spirit of God indwells us, we also have the character of the Spirit within us. As the Spirit is patient, so we also have patience. If you don't feel like you have patience, it is because you have tried to find it in yourself. Our choice to rely on God is the key.

Part of our reliance on God is to stick to His revealed plan. When we ask for wisdom and God gives us a pathway to the answer, we must make note, write it down (so we do not forget it), and then stick to the plan. Oftentimes the pathway to the answer is given to us through a momentary glimpse, and then the clouds of life obscure it once again. During that glimpse, we must take a "compass reading" to know what we are to do and then stick to the heading/plan that we have.

Like a pilot flying by instruments or a captain sailing through fog or darkness, use the knowledge you gain when Christ reveals His presence and trust Him enough to walk to Him. He does not mislead. Even though Peter could see Christ beckoning him to walk on water, and he was successfully doing that, the waves and wind around him broke his concentration and he began to sink. Remember Christ's calling when you see clearly and "stay the course." He is not only waiting for you, He is with you every step of the way!

Second Chances Are Seldom Clean

Second chances are seldom clean. Life is messy. All of us have hot spots, sore spots, and spots we like to keep covered as a result of previous losses. On the positive side, we can develop emotional and spiritual muscle, but by the time we have gained much experience in life, we usually have scars as well. Those scars are manifested in a variety of issues ranging from inconvenience to real adversity: loss of the comfort of the familiar due to change of location or career, children in a blended family, emotional scars from past abuse, fear, physical limitations from illness or injury, etc. Whether mild pressure points or real sore spots, they can create hardship as we move forward.

These issues cannot be ignored, but neither do they need to control you. God's infinite wisdom and knowledge is essential for coping successfully. Each pathway is different, but He knows the way, and He will be faithful to lead you through it.

When facing the scars of past mistakes, the lesson we need to learn is perseverance. God's grace means that we are not defined by our mistakes – however the world tries to hold us captive by them. Learn to separate truth from fear. Fear will hold you hostage, but in God's truth we find freedom.

When your decisions hurt other people, their pain and loss can become your scars as well. The challenge is to know when someone else's issues are not binding on you. Just like you, everyone must do the work of bringing their choices into line with God's will for them. When people try to make you responsible for correcting problems only they can remedy, you can choose not to accept responsibility.

Everybody has an agenda. Often people use guilt to manipulate others to do their will. God does not motivate by guilt, so if guilt is the driving factor behind whether or not you get involved, then your motivation has been hijacked by someone or something other than God.

> Look past the problem in order to focus on the solution. The solution is not the circumstance you are in, it is beyond them.

When someone knocks on your door, use the peephole. If what is being offered is not yours, don't open the door or accept the package. It may be useful to think of a ready response in advance, one that will give you time to evaluate the situation. You must discern God's intentions for you and stay focused on them.

Moving forward by God's Spirit takes courage and forward thinking. Our success and ability to respond – instead of react – to issues is an outgrowth of a nourished soul (fruit of the Spirit). You must defend your God-approved priorities.

In *The Tyranny of the Urgent* Charles E. Hummel says, "Your greatest danger is letting the urgent things crowd out the important." The struggle is in knowing the difference between what is urgent and what is important. Only by understanding what God is calling you to, and where He is calling you, can you discern the important. And once again, when God reveals His plan to us, on that we must stay focused.

The movie *Patch Adams* is based on the true story of Dr. Hunter Adam. Early in his adult life, Patch commits himself to a West Virginia Mental Institution because of his deep depression. While in the hospital, Patch begins to learn that the pathway to healing himself is by helping others. In the movie, Patch meets the fictional character Arthur Mendelson (a rich, intelligent, and eccentric multimillionaire) who challenges everyone around him with a seemingly ludicrous riddle. He extends four fingers on his hand and asks everyone how many fingers he is holding up. When they answer four he becomes agitated. When Patch asks him why he gets so agitated, Arthur tells him, "Look beyond my hand. Now what do you see?" As Patch looks beyond his hand, his eyes lose focus on Arthur's hand and his eyes perceive eight fingers instead. Arthur goes on to say, "That's right! Eight is a good number! Look beyond the problem. See things that others can't see. See things that others choose not to see!"

This is good instruction for us as well. We must look past the problem in order to focus on the solution. The solution is not the circumstance you are in, it is beyond them. It is not that God is not with us in our problems; it is that our future and second chances lie beyond our current circumstances. That is why Christ calls us from beyond our circumstances.

How do we recognize and acknowledge our second chances? How do we get from here to there? We look to God; we lay our lives at the foot of the cross of Jesus and wait for His Spirit to lead us step by step. We learn from our past and allow Him to build our future. Too simple? Not the answer you were looking for? Christ is the key to choosing the right door, and Christ is the key to opening it.

For Discussion/Reflection:
- What choices are you facing?
- What issues are making it difficult for you to know which door to go through?
- What does patience look like to you?
- How can you prevent "jumping the gun" on God's timing?

Prayer to Understand Your Opportunities

Heavenly Father, thank you for the gift of second chances. Help me to understand what my choices are and when to move forward into them. Grant me patience to wait for the right time and opportunity; give me a discerning spirit to know when to act and what door to choose. May the choices I make be pleasing to You, Oh Lord. In Jesus' name, Amen.

CHAPTER FIVE

DEFINING MOMENTS

Now that we have laid the groundwork of the "open door," the opportunity of a second chance, we need to look at something that often accompanies a second chance. That is "A Defining Moment."

Defining Moment: noun

> a point at which the essential nature or character of a perso
> n, group, etc., is revealed or identified.

When it comes to second chances, a defining moment is that time when you finally learn who you are and who God is. At some point, God reveals a part of His character through a revelation in our lives. It is an experience that is hard to define because it is so unique to each person, but you will know when it occurs, or shortly thereafter. Above all else, a defining moment is a crossroad at which we surrender ourselves. It is the place where we end and a place where we allow God to set the direction for our lives. God begins.

It is possible to experience a defining moment and not grasp it at the time. Although defining moments can be subtler, they reach so deep inside of us and our spirit that it is not uncommon to feel overwhelmed and even confused at first. It is also a very humbling experience. As you begin to sense the real magnitude of who God is and what He does, as well as what He is capable of, it is very common to sense your own weakness and insufficiency before Him.

Strong emotions frequently accompany a defining moment experience. You may feel contrasting feelings simultaneously. You may sense both joy and sadness, fear and peace, or boldness and timidity, along with many other feelings. For instance, you may feel joy at the realization that Jesus has been victorious over your failure, but also saddened by the conviction that your failure to trust the Lord or walk out His calling on your life ended in your first loss. There is no question that these seemingly conflicting emotions may lead to a sense of confusion about what is going on, but because it is a movement of the Holy Spirit within us, the sense of confusion will quickly give way to indescribable peace, joy, confidence, and often resolve.

> One of the greatest mistakes we make, the one that leads to most lost firsts, is when we take control of opportunities in our lives that we are incapable of managing without God.

In order to understand what a defining moment really is, it is necessary to understand who the Holy Spirit is and how He works in us. The Bible teaches us that, although God is one being, He consists of three persons: Father, Son, and Holy Spirit. For lack of a better way to describe Him, we use the title "Trinity." Each of the persons is known for a specific function of God's character. The Father is known as the Creator; the Son, Jesus, is known as the Redeemer (the One who paid the price to buy us back from our sin); and the Holy Spirit is our Guide and Counselor.

It is the Holy Spirit who convicts us (never condemns us). The Holy Spirit is also the One who reveals the character of God to us. Therefore, the defining moment comes as the result of the Holy Spirit breaking through and connecting with our spirit to reveal a deep truth about who God is and what He has done – and will do – in our lives.

> "But I tell you the truth, it is to your advantage that I go
> away; for if I do not go away, the Helper will not come to

you; but if I go, I will send Him to you. "And He, when He comes, will convict the world concerning sin and righteousness and judgment; ... I have many more things to say to you, but you cannot bear them now. But when He, the Spirit of truth, comes, He will guide you into all the truth; for He will not speak on His own initiative, but whatever He hears, He will speak; and He will disclose to you what is to come." (John 16:7-8, 12-13)

By Jesus' very definition of the Holy Spirit, we discover that we must be Spirit-filled and Spirit-led in order to understand the truths of God necessary for breakthroughs to occur and for us to be victorious in our lives. The Holy Spirit moves us, through defining moments, to an essential understanding of the role and importance of total surrender to God in our lives.

One of the greatest mistakes we make, the one that leads to most lost firsts, is when we take control of opportunities in our lives that we are incapable of managing without God. The natural assumption of mankind is: "If I don't do it, nobody will do it for me." While there is truth to that statement when it comes to being diligent, it is also very misleading when it comes to determining our purpose and managing our lives. We often do not even know what is happening to us when it happens, let alone what will occur in the future. We can plan our lives, but only God knows the future and what is needed to navigate through what is to come. Thus, you can only thrive when you surrender, and you can only surrender when the Holy Spirit inspires you.

Additionally, a defining moment results in a significant change of direction in your spiritual life. Obviously, the change from not being a believer in God to accepting Jesus as your Lord and Savior would be the most radical change. But you do not have to be an unbeliever to have a defining moment and significant change in your spiritual direction. Many who have grown up in church cannot remember a time when they didn't know God was, but they are able to recall a defining moment when that knowledge became alive, an experience that impacted them in such a way that it changed the way they looked at life forever.

For you, it may be a time when Jesus goes from being just your Savior (a way to get to heaven) to your Lord (walking with you every day to direct, guide, and bless you). It changes your perspective and thus the way you look at your problems, options, and responsibilities. When the Spirit reveals the character of God in your life, you will be able to see things the way Christ sees them.

A defining moment could take the form of a miracle or a miraculous healing. It could be the result of the birth of a child or at seeing the vastness and magnitude of God's creation. It may come from a worship experience in which the Holy Spirit touches you deeply, or the result of something profound being revealed to you in God's Word. It may be something you experience alone in the presence of God. It could come as the result of God using someone to expose you to His Truth.

We are not limited to one defining moment. For most of us there will be a number of defining moments. Your first may come when you accept Christ as your Savior, lay down your efforts to drive your life, and ask for God's guidance. But there may be many other moments in your life when God reveals to you another truth about Himself; they occur as you master what God has revealed and are ready to learn and apply a new truth.

Defining moments inspire us to a new passion and zeal in life. They have the power to cause you to take a radical new direction. They can inspire you to an act of forgiveness beyond what you believed you were capable of. They have the power to break an addiction. They kindle the fire of passion for life and purpose because you can see that what God is calling you to is attainable.

In every case we learn that God did not suddenly appear. We see that God has been there, seen or unseen, all along. He has been wooing us, beckoning to us, calling us to open our hearts to Him. Even as He reveals Himself to us in these defining moments, whether through supernatural signs and wonders or through the revelation and application of His Word, we always come away with the understanding that He has never left us.

Defining moments can be contagious. The fire and zeal that flow from defining moments are seldom containable. You have an almost uncontrollable desire to share your experience or insight with those around you. When you start to understand just how big God is and His Spirit indwells within you, you can no more contain Him than a covered pot can contain the steam from boiling water. His joy is uncontainable, and this is the best starting place for a second chance!

Lessons from the Woman at the Well
The Bible is filled with examples of defining moments:

- Elisha's servant seeing the horses and chariots of fire (2 Kings 6:17)
- the Transformation of Jesus on the high mountain (Matthew 17:1-9)
- the Day of Pentecost (Acts 2:1-13)

One of our favorite defining moments is found at the well of a small Samaritan town called Sychar at midday (John 4:1-42).

The story is most frequently known as the story of "The Woman at The Well." It came about while Jesus was travelling with his disciples to Jerusalem and passing through Samaria, an area between Galilee and Judea. Samaria was populated by people who were the remnant of the northern tribes of Israel and considered by the Jews as compromisers and undesirables.

While Jesus was resting at a well, as the disciples went into town for food, a woman approached the well to draw water. While a woman drawing water is not unusual, the time of day that she went was. Because the well would have been a social gathering place, her timing suggests that she was a social outcast.

Jesus speaks to her and asks her for a drink of water, which was also unusual as rarely did a Jew interact with a Samaritan. Through the course of the dialogue Jesus redirects her from a discussion of physical water to the subject of "spiritual water" (salvation). To exemplify His authority to speak, Jesus reveals facts about the woman's personal life that she would not have expected many to know (she had been married 5 times and was living with her current partner).

In the remainder of the dialogue Jesus discloses Himself as the Messiah, and by so doing, He inspires her to leave her water and run back to town to tell everyone about whom she had met and the things He told her. The townspeople respond by coming out to meet Jesus for themselves and, after several days of ministry, the story ends with this verse:

> "We no longer believe just because of what you said; now we have heard for ourselves, and we know that this man really is the Savior of the world." (John 4:42)

What do we learn from this story about defining moments? First, we learn that Jesus meets us where we are.

> "Jacob's well was there, and Jesus, tired as he was from the journey, sat down by the well. It was about noon. When a Samaritan woman came to draw water, Jesus said to her, 'Will you give me a drink?'" (John 4:6-7)

It was Jesus who found the woman not the other way around. When the disciples went into town to get food, He stayed behind to be available to meet the woman when she came. Notice also that, of all of the people who lived in that town, Jesus chose this woman. Why? Because He knew this woman's heart, her desire, and the passion she would have to share what He was about to teach her. He also knew that, in that community, her testimony would be the most effective in spreading the truth about the Messiah.

Being people who naturally prefer to control so much of our lives, we automatically assume that we have to "go find Jesus." The truth is, we don't find Him, He finds us. In the same way He did with the woman, Jesus waits for us so that we will not miss Him. On our own, we don't even know enough to look for Jesus. Even if we did, we'd have no idea where to find Him, except for the guiding of His Spirit. Even as believers, we don't "find" Jesus when we need Him; He never leaves us and stands ready to meet us in those precious divine appointments.

Even the Lord's timing is not random. Not only does Jesus find us and meet us, His timing is strategic to offer us the greatest advantage of our encounter with Him. This is also why there is a deep sense of conviction that comes with a divine appointment; even though it may seem that some encounters with the Lord come when we are far away from Him, the truth is that His Spirit has already paved the way for us to hear His message and respond to it.

Divine appointments often lead to defining moments.

Think about this: Jesus called the woman at the well when she was by herself – she was collecting water at midday, when no one else was around. Most women collected water in the cool of the day and it was a social event. It is most apparent that she was a social outcast. Jesus knew when and where to reach her. Christ's divine appointments are often when no one else is around and when we are just going about the daily routine of life. The apostle Matthew was working at his tax booth; Peter, James, and John were mending nets or fishing; Andrew was at a revival with John the Baptist; Nathan was under a tree, relaxing; God called Samuel in the middle of the night. Divine appointments which lead to defining moments can occur just about anywhere, but they will always be when Jesus knows He can best connect with you.

It doesn't matter where you are today. It doesn't matter if you have reached the goals that you set for yourself. Today, Jesus sees you where you are, and He will meet you. He's not counting on His fingers how many times you failed or succeeded. He is watching for a heart that will be open to a defining moment and the second chance that will come from it. He's most assuredly waiting for you at the well to show you who He is and what He has for in store for you.

Next, it is not what we bring to the encounter that matters, but what God brings.

> "…How can you ask me for a drink?" (For Jews do not associate with Samaritans)

> "Jesus answered her, 'If you knew the gift of God and who it is that asks you for a drink, you would have asked him and he would have given you living water.'" (John 4:9-10)

Jesus came to the woman at the well to offer a gift. He is rich in resources. He is our provider and supplies all our needs. When Jesus and the woman began to discuss water, the woman thought she was prepared and Jesus was not. When He told her that she should ask Him for water, she thought the idea was foolish; He did not have a bucket to draw with. The subject of "water" was inconsequential and served only as a catalyst for Him to speak to her about salvation.

When Jesus reveals a truth to our spirit that never occurred to us before (and/or others have not seen), we are changed. Consider the encounter with the woman. The conversation started with her sufficiency (to draw water) and Jesus' insufficiency to do the same. This became a defining moment when she recognized her insufficiency to find salvation and Jesus' sufficiency to bring salvation to her. The defining moment came when Jesus revealed that He was the "Living Water" and the way to salvation.

God orchestrates our future plans when we turn our lives over to Him. He brings hope to those without hope. He brings value to those who have no value by the world's standards. He brings healing to those who are broken-hearted. He brings forgiveness to those who are buried by sin and guilt. If we can't see things happening, it doesn't mean He isn't working. God will take every opportunity to meet with us – when our hearts are ready, and we are willing to become a follower.

Divine appointments often lead to defining moments. Jesus will meet us where we are and will take what is important to us and turn it into an opportunity to speak into our very spirit. We may believe we possess the resources to address our (perceived) needs, but it is God who meets our deepest, most critical needs. It is He who changes our lives and opens the door to second chances in those precious moments when He shows us something about who He is that will forever change our perspective on life and priorities.

The third truth is that Jesus speaks the truth in love.

> "He told her, 'Go, call your husband and come back.' 'I have no husband,' she replied. Jesus said to her, 'You are right when you say you have no husband. The fact is, you have had five husbands, and the man you now have is not your husband. What you have just said is quite true.' 'Sir,' the woman said, 'I can see that you are a prophet.'" (John 4:17-19)

He caused her to look more closely at her own life and her own issues. The evidence of His character was found in His ability to reveal aspects of her life, but it was His acceptance of her despite the issues of her life, and the hope for attainable salvation, that changed her life.

Many theologians and pastors have taught that the woman at the well was a woman of loose morals because she had five husbands. The truth is, we really don't know what the circumstances were regarding her five former marriages. They may have ended in divorce, but if so, as a woman, she probably would not have been capable of initiating the divorce. She could have been widowed any number of times, which would have carried the title "cursed" by the others in the village. She undoubtedly had a bit of an attitude by the way she responded to Jesus' initial request and subsequent comments. If she was a person of loose morals, it probably would not have been a surprise to the people of the village that Jesus was able to tell her about her history. Every gossip in town could have told you all about the dirt on her. I believe her history would not have been common knowledge or it would have been no surprise that Jesus or anyone else would know all about her. The people responded to the testimony that Jesus knew things about her that no one should have known.

> "Many of the Samaritans from that town believed in him because of the woman's testimony, 'He told me everything I ever did.'" (John 4:39)

The impact of that witness brought the entire town out to meet Jesus.

Any way you look at it, Jesus met her where she was. He patiently overcame her doubt, skepticism, and maybe sarcasm, and He spoke acceptance to her and showed her a pathway beyond her history. Likewise, He continues to offer us hope and a new opportunity, a new direction, and maybe at times even a "re-do." He accepts who we are and offers a way past what we have done or what has been done to us. It has been said that "Jesus loves us where we are, but He loves us enough not to leave us there."

Jesus modeled true love and friendship to the woman at the well by speaking the truth in love. In a day and age where the world says that a real friend accepts us *and* our behavior, we often hold back the truth for fear of offending someone. We may justify our silence by saying that we just want to "encourage" the other person. The fact is, we have done just the opposite. Truth takes boldness and is required by love. Those who choose to tell the truth in love can walk a lonely road next to the highway of today's generalized acceptance. There is always the chance of rejection, but we need to move past being popular and strive to be truthful. Spiritual lives depend on it. Jesus takes that chance for us, and when we accept His truth, we often find a defining moment in that revelation.

Lastly, Jesus inspired the woman at the well, and she told everyone about their meeting and the things He told her.

> "Then, leaving her water jar, the woman went back to the town and said to the people, 'Come, see a man who told me everything I ever did. Could this be the Messiah?' They came out of the town and made their way toward him." (John 4:28-30)

The Bible tells us that she left the water jar there and ran to tell everyone else what she had found in Jesus. The woman was so excited about what she had learned that she simply could not contain her enthusiasm, nor could she wait to tell others. Who knows when she finally remembered to take the water home?

Jesus will always meet you where you are.

When Jesus meets with us in a defining moment we cannot contain it. We are inspired even when He reveals our faults because of the freedom it brings us. No longer do we have to carry a burden of guilt, false responsibility, excuses, lies, and facades. When He moves and makes an impact on our lives, we are compelled to talk to others – to share our freedom, our revelations, our peace or joy.

Even more than that, we are compelled to live out the truth of who God is in our lives. It doesn't just change the words we say, but also our perspective: how we view life, the way we think, and the way we act – toward God, toward others, and toward ourselves. The presence of God within us cannot and will not be contained. When we walk out what the Lord has done in our lives, the Fruit of His Spirit becomes evident in us.

> "But the fruit of the Spirit is love, joy, peace, forbearance, kindness, goodness, faithfulness, gentleness and self-control." (Galatians: 5:22-23)

The Fruit of the Spirit compels us and empowers us to LIVE OUT LOUD.

Lessons from Saul's Conversion

Another of our favorite defining moments was the conversion of Saul, who was later to go by his Roman name Paul, who had a much more dramatic defining moment with God. God had plans to move him from an adversary of Christ to, arguably, the greatest evangelist for Christ the world has ever known. It was because God could see into Saul's heart that he knew of his heart for God. The problem was, Saul was living it out in the ignorance and darkness of the world. As a Pharisee, he was living his life under the Law as he was taught by those in authority over him. He was persecuting those who followed Jesus Christ. The required change in his life would have to be dramatic, and God would make his defining moment equally dramatic.

It is important to note that Saul/Paul's defining moment was no deeper or more intimate than the woman at the well or anyone else's defining moment. God may use different methods, but His goal is always the same: to bring us into a deeper understanding of Himself, and to prepare us for our second chance.

To summarize Saul's story from Acts 9:1-9, 17-22:

> Saul was a young Pharisee (a major religious sect who held great influence and power over the Jewish people). As a zealot for his cause, Saul requested and was granted permission to pursue and imprison Christians for their faith. While on the way to Damascus, Syria, Jesus intervened and confronted Saul in the form of a blinding light and loud voice, asking "Saul, why do you persecute Me?"

> Saul, broken by his encounter with Christ, continued as directed to Syria to meet with a disciple named Ananias. After 3 days of being blind and fasting, he met with Ananias who laid hands on him. He was filled with the Holy Spirit and regained his sight. From that point on, he began to witness to the truth of Jesus as the Messiah and was able to use his knowledge and training to confound the Jewish leader with his proof.

What do we learn from Paul's "Damascus Road Experience?"

A defining moment sometimes involves God intervening in a dramatic fashion.

> "As he neared Damascus on his journey, suddenly a light from heaven flashed around him. He fell to the ground and heard a voice say to him, 'Saul, Saul, why do you persecute me?'" (Acts 9:3-4)

Often God does this to get the attention of those who are farther away or are more passionate in their opposition to Christ. There is no preparing for an encounter like this.

It is important to note that Paul was not looking for an encounter with God at all. That was part of the problem. Paul did not realize that Christ was the God he was trying to serve. Christ needed to make this defining moment unmistakably clear so that Paul would get the message – whether he was seeking it or not.

Another example of this transformation is the great theologian and reformer Martin Luther. He was studying to be a lawyer when he met God in the middle of a lightning storm. Later, while searching for God in the Scriptures, God met Luther in a subtler defining moment, when he discovered the truth of "Salvation, by grace through faith, not by works...." This truth became the inspiration for the reformation of the church.

If we only look for dramatic moments, we will miss the subtler ways that God moves most frequently. It is much more common for God to move through the tender guidance of those who are already seeking Him. Consider the prophet Elijah on Mount Sinai who was looking for God in the dramatic – fire, wind, or earthquake. He found God in a gentle breeze. While we don't need to rely on a dramatic defining moment, we cannot be afraid of the dramatic either. Especially when we are looking for an encounter with God, we must be open to either method.

Another thing we learn through Saul's defining moment is that the encounter can involve a breaking of our pride and independence.

"Saul got up from the ground, but when he opened his eyes he could see nothing. So they led him by the hand into Damascus. For three days he was blind and did not eat or drink anything." (Acts 9:8-9)

Saul was very confident of his knowledge and motives. He was, in his own words, a "Pharisee of Pharisees." He was zealous in pursuit of his legalistic self-righteousness and had compartmentalized any behavior that might challenge his perception of self-righteousness. But confidence and zeal do not make things right.

Just because you are confident and zealous in your beliefs does not mean that they are pleasing to God or are leading to everlasting life. I am reminded of a turn on the cliché "Practice makes perfect" that my former swim coach always used to say: "Practice makes permanent." What was he saying? Practice does not itself guarantee success. If you practice a bad habit long enough, you will get good at doing the wrong thing and it will be more difficult to make the change needed to be successful. We must practice the right things.

> God can turn the zeal of our rebellion into the passion for our second chances.

God may need to break the bad habits of pride and independence so that we can have a relationship with Him or fulfill His call on our lives. When defining moments break us of pride, we can finally learn to be at peace, content with being in the center of His will. It is here that we awaken to the changes needed if we are to be ready to move out when He calls. When we are humble and teachable, there may not be a need for an earthquake to gain our attention. But when we are living in our own strength and self-will, going about life without conviction or care (or even in opposition to God's direction), a more dramatic defining moment may be needed to tear down the pride and independence that is blocking our pathway to God and where He wants us to be. This is what the Bible says about an encounter with Christ:

"Anyone who falls on this stone will be broken to pieces; anyone on whom it falls will be crushed." (Matthew 21:44)

Saul honestly thought he was doing right by killing Christians. Though later in life he refers to himself as the "chief of sinners" for his actions, he did not knowingly seek to put himself above God and His people. He was not deliberately self-serving, intentionally denying God His place on the throne. His motivation was good, but he'd become hardened to the Truth. When Christ revealed Himself to Saul as the "stone the builders rejected which has become the Cornerstone," Saul fell on it and was broken. In his brokenness God was able to reshape him for his incredible second chance.

It's also important to note that dramatic moves do not necessarily come because of rebellion or because of purposeful sin in our lives. God will be the one to determine when and where a dramatic intervention occurs. We cannot wrap our minds around God's plan and purpose; therefore, we must be content to know that He is a good Father, and His ways are higher than ours.

The third lesson from the story of Saul's conversion is that God can turn the zeal of our rebellion into the passion for our second chances.

"Yet Saul grew more and more powerful and baffled the Jews living in Damascus by proving that Jesus is the Messiah." (Acts 9:22)

Saul's zeal as a Pharisee was evidence of what a passionate person he was. Once he was redirected, Paul went on to become the apostle to the Gentiles and the most effective evangelist in history – but God had to be especially forceful to turn all that intensity in the right direction.

The more passionately we pursue a wrong direction in our lives, the more dramatic God's intervention may have to be to get our attention. The Holy Spirit has the power to redirect our passion. God made us and placed within us certain passions, enabled us with particular gifts. Our passions and gifts help define us, set us apart. But they must be used for God's purposes to be good and effective. Defining moments often redirect our zeal and enthusiasm so that we can apply them to the fulfillment of God's purpose.

I (John) am reminded of a toy I had when I was young. You can still find it today. It's called Newton's Cradle. It's a simple framework with five steel balls suspended in a perfect line within the frame. Here's how the toy works: The player pulls back one or more of the balls and then releases them. When the swinging balls strike the stationary ball(s), the exact same number of balls will swing out in the opposite direction. If two balls are pulled back and released, two balls on the opposite side of the stack will swing out. If three balls are pulled and released, three will swing out, and so forth. The toy is meant to demonstrate Newton's three laws of motion, but for our purposes it can illustrate the transfer of passion. Just as with the steel balls in Newton's Cradle, God can use our misdirected zeal to create an equally passion-filled second chance – sometimes in an opposite direction.

Misdirected does not necessarily mean rebellious. Sometimes zealous, passionate people just charge out ahead of God's call and direction. Sometimes he saves us. Other times, He lets us run. We may find our defining moment when we are at the end of our rope, and there is nothing left for us to do but to look up to Him.

Unfortunately, most passionate people do not choose to learn from others before they strike out on their own. Many of our most passionate leaders have come through times of passionate rebellion, presumption, or failure, but God uses them nonetheless to do great things. These are people whose very witness may well be the distance that God has moved them from where they were to where they are today.

It is very important to understand that a moment with God does not have to be dramatic to be defining. There is a real danger in missing opportunities because you don't see and accept them as such; they didn't seem dramatic enough. But I will go out on a limb and say that, most likely, if you are close enough in your walk with

God to be "looking" for Him to act dramatically, then He probably doesn't need to be dramatic. Look instead for more subtle defining moments that may do more in your life. While a dramatic moment might be necessary to get the attention of someone who is far away from God, He may be able to connect with you on a deeper level in a subtle way to empower you to move forward.

Meeting Jesus Face to Face

At the very heart of a defining moment is the reality that Jesus still meets people face to face. I will be so bold as to say that there will be at least one defining moment in the life of every person. That is not to say that you will be physically swept up to heaven and stand before Jesus, but that in a very real way Jesus will reveal Himself to you and connect with your spirit. Even unbelievers will have defining moments, though they may not attribute them to God or accept the invitation to draw close to Him.

You can count on meeting Jesus face to face whether through His Word, a miraculous event (e.g., inexplicable physical healing, birth of a child, an answered prayer), or even a Damascus Road redirection experience. Here, during these moments, is where we begin to see change – a milestone marking change. Either our hearts are hardened against God, or His character is revealed to us in our submission and awe toward Him.

Although I have had a few defining moments in my life, none have made as big an impact as my experience in Kazakhstan. Let me tell you about that:

After high school, I attended the University of Florida with the intent to be an engineer, but God had other plans for me. By the end of my sophomore year I had my first defining moment when I heard God's call on me to go into full-time pastoral ministry. Following my graduation, I went on to seminary where I studied and interned over a four-year period to prepare to serve as a pastor. The Lutheran education was very thorough theologically, but encounters with God and revelations of His character cannot be taught in a classroom.

For the first 12 years of my professional life, I was an ordained pastor in full-time ministry in the Lutheran Church. Ten years into my ministry, I had the opportunity to join a group of ministry experts on a "missionary support" trip to Almaty, Kazakhstan. It was the first time I had ever gone on a mission trip outside of the United States. Leave it to God to make my first trip halfway around the world to make sure that He would have my undivided attention. This was just a few years after the fall of the Iron Curtain. Kazakhstan had been a part of the former Soviet Union.

In the years following the opening of the borders, missionaries went into the various former Soviet countries and started preaching and teaching the Word. In that time God began doing a miraculous work, and many thousands of people came to the Lord. Many of the newly-saved returned to their hometowns as missionaries themselves. As God blessed their efforts, there arose a need for additional training to empower these new missionaries to lead their growing congregations. This is where our group came in. We went to teach these people, but in my case, I learned that God was sending me there so I could learn through them.

When our flight landed, I knew we "weren't in Kansas anymore." I looked out the window. All over the tarmac, soldiers in green military uniforms carried automatic weapons. We disembarked from the plane and entered customs, where almost everyone spoke a language I could not understand. I was barely able to greet anyone, let alone have a conversation. I was already way out of my comfort zone and safety zone. I had to trust that God had it from there.

We held a week-long leadership development conference for indigenous pastors. They came from four or five countries in the region, many travelling for days to get to the conference. Toward the end of the week, God did something amazing that would forever shape my future. The local people celebrated May Day holiday, which was similar to our Labor Day, a time to celebrate the working people. The locals had asked if we could break off the seminar early so that we could spend the afternoon praying for each of the people groups represented at the conference. Over the next few hours representatives from several countries and over 20 different people groups came forward to pray for their people. I was fascinated by the diversity of cultures: Russians, Chinese, Mongolian, Kazakhs. There were people who could trace their ancestry to German POWs who never went home after the war and a nomadic people who claimed to trace their lineage to the Assyrians of Old Testament times.

Dear Lord, please don't leave me on the sidelines, but put me in the game when you move!

During the time of prayer, an individual stood up to represent the people of Uzbekistan. I didn't think much of it at the time, although we were asked not to take any pictures of him; the Muslims of Uzbekistan had placed a bounty on him because of his work as a Christian missionary. An educated individual, he had received the Lord some years earlier and had begun to evangelize the people from his country, ministering to them in small groups because Christianity was unacceptable. He had to keep a low profile.

The man told us of being arrested and imprisoned, as well as the high price some of the members of his congregation had paid for professing Jesus as Lord and Savior. Even his presence at the meeting that week came at great cost. His life was at risk due to the death threats against him. A court ruling on Christian freedom was pending back home; an unfavorable ruling would prohibit him from ever returning to the country – and to his wife, who was facing a severe health issue. The man believed God had called him to be at that conference, and he was obedient to His call. His prayers were for God to intervene in all three of those areas of his life and ministry.

Now, as a Lutheran, I considered myself a good preacher and an eloquent leader of prayer. I was a very good wordsmith. I recognized that this ability was a gift from God, and I truly desired to use it to please Him and serve Him. What I didn't know was "what I didn't know." In my ignorance, I had been asking God to act without ever really believing He would do anything about it, except for occasionally healing someone under a doctor's care. I would end my prayers with "Your will be done." That sounded pious, but it was really a "disclaimer" so that if/when God did not grant the request, I could simply say, "it wasn't God's will." Believing God still answered prayer with miracles was the arena of the radical charismatics and was to be avoided. God was about to change that view dramatically the next day.

We concluded that May Day evening with the time of prayer, and I didn't think a whole lot more about any of it. The next day, as we gathered together for the final session of the seminar, the room was all abuzz. Since they were speaking in Russian, I could not understand what they were talking about, so I found an interpreter. They were so excited about whatever was going on that he asked me to wait until the end of the announcements to explain it all to me. He didn't want to miss anything. Finally, he told me that Word had come; God had answered our prayers for Uzbekistan. The court had ruled in favor of the Christians' right to public assembly and had refunded them all of the fines that had been levied against them. What is more, the pastor's wife had been healed. I was stunned! I had never experienced anything like that before. There is power in prayer. God still does the miraculous.

It took me over a month to process what had happened that day, but through it, God changed my understanding of His character and my view of serving Him. I would never be able to look at prayer the same way again. I would forever be empowered by the knowledge that God meets us in prayer and can "bring down mountains and raise valleys." I learned that, through prayer, we have power over the enemy.

We do not simply have to accept "fate." God is so much bigger than fate. Many things would happen to me in the wake of that day, many more "Lost Firsts" that would lead to opportunities for a second chance – all shaped by that defining moment in Kazakhstan.

Before all of this began, the Holy Spirit had placed the seed in me that there was more to this life and my ministry than I was experiencing – and more than I understood. I remember praying, "Dear Lord, I know you are about to do something incredible in this world. I know that you are about to move and I want to be 'in the game.' Please don't leave me on the sidelines, but put me in the game when you move." I had many ideas about what my involvement would look like, but God knew where He wanted me. To that end, He used a defining moment to prepare me for a day like today and a time like now.

Characteristics of Defining Moments

In hindsight, there will be no mistaking the fact that you have been through a defining moment. However, there are characteristics of these moments that may help you to understand when you are in them and how to make the most of them while you are there. Certain circumstances help to shape your heart to be ready to receive the revelation that God will give you in a defining moment. They do not all apply to every defining moment experience, but every defining moment has at least one of these characteristics.

The first is brokenness. In 2 Corinthians 12:9 Paul talks about a defining moment for him. Paul is struggling with a personal issue. He never says what the issue is, but whatever it is, he is very frustrated with his perceived impact on his ministry.

But he said to me, "My grace is sufficient for you, for my power is made perfect in weakness." Therefore I will boast all the more gladly about my weaknesses, so that Christ's power may rest on me.

In the brokenness of his weakness, Paul was able to truly experience the revelation of God's power.

This is not to say that brokenness is the same as being dysfunctional or unstable. The brokenness that I am referring to is a spiritual brokenness. It is the breaking of our pride and coming to a place of humility. Some who have been overcome, whether by their first loss or a current crisis, need healing before they are ready for a defining moment. Jesus "binds the broken-hearted" before He takes them deeper and empowers them.

Brokenness that paves the way for a defining moment is not always the result of God "breaking our pride." Brokenness may be due to circumstances: consequences we face for poor choices we have made in our past or situations we endure that are not of our own doing. For a spiritually mature person, brokenness can be brought about through fasting. We can humble ourselves before the Lord, especially in times of urgency or crisis, so as to be open for God to reveal Himself.

The next is maturity. The ability to hear God in the quiet, subtle times is a sign of spiritual maturity. God will not need to "get our attention" in a defining way if we abide with Him every day through a close personal relationship. There is nothing wrong with waiting expectantly for God to reveal Himself in a defining way. It is just that, if that is your focus, there is a good chance you might miss the many ways God offers you guidance and direction. If we live for the defining moment, we run the risk of mentally and emotionally defining that moment and revelation *for* God. Instead of listening for God to reveal what He wants in the way He wants, we create images, expectations, and even walls to protect our epiphany. When God is reaching to us and we do not expect it, there is less resistance and more openness to accept what God Himself is saying.

A third possible characteristic of a defining moment is divine intervention. I (Jerri) was under a great deal of stress in my young adulthood. I had taken on many responsibilities which I have listed earlier. Most of these responsibilities were not supposed to be mine to take. At that time, I was going to nursing school. It was common for me to experience episodes of rapid heartbeats brought on by anxiety. In addition to being stressed, I was fearful of these episodes. I found myself focused on them. Soon it became an obsession. I would take my pulse any time I thought I felt my heart skip a beat – which was often.

One night I was taking my pulse while lying in bed in a quiet house. I should have been sleeping, but I found myself awake, fretting over the irregular heartbeats I was experiencing. A feeling of impending doom overwhelmed me. I was gripped by fear. Suddenly, a blinding white light appeared in the corner of my room. I felt I heard God's voice. I also noted that, although I was still clutching the pulse at my wrist, I had not felt one heartbeat. I moved my hand from my wrist to my throat and still felt no pulse. Then I "heard" God say that life and death were in the power of His hands, not mine. It was as if He had come into my room that night. I was awestruck. I wanted to slide out of bed and get on my face, but I was too overcome to move. Before I could think further, the light went away. Once again I could feel my pulse. From that moment on, I knew God had control of my life, and I was compelled to stop obsessing over my heart rate. This was definitely a defining moment for me. I was challenged to trust Him for my life – daily.

God still can and does intervene in the lives of His children today. There are many who tell of miraculous healings or being spared certain death. The most important thing to know about these kinds of defining moments is that it is not *what* God did that we need to focus on, but rather *why* He did it. What was He trying to teach you about Himself? In my case, he wanted me to know that I needed to trust Him for life and not look to myself or my fears for guidance.

The fourth characteristic of defining moments is revelation. If, as a result of an encounter with God, you come away saying "Aha," then you may have had a defining moment. "Aha" moments are when you have an encounter with some word or promise from God and you see a truth about Him in it that you have not seen before. This is when Logos (the word/knowledge) becomes Ramos (living/relational).

Not every "Aha" moment is a defining moment. The closer we are to God, the more He reveals Himself to us every day. The revelation intended here so impacts us as to change our very outlook, attitude, or action. This leads us to the last characteristic that I want to share: lasting effect.

A defining moment has an impact that leaves a lasting effect on us. We are not – cannot be – the same person as the result of this encounter and revelation. It results in a change of thought, attitude, actions, and possibly in our very character. Our defining moment is the day we accept Jesus as Lord, the change results in a profession of faith and the desire to leave any sinful behaviors behind and commit to a sanctified lifestyle. For those who are already Christ-followers, changes may include (but are not limited to) letting go of fears, humbling themselves, becoming more teachable, and taking God-inspired risks.

> Discovering your insufficiency may even be the object of your defining moment.

Change is a natural reaction to a defining moment. It is by the power of His Holy Spirit that we are compelled to change. If we do not change, God doesn't give up on us. Usually the spiritual and emotional consequences become overwhelming until we yield to Him. This is not something to fear. He sees all things and knows what is best for us. His promise is that:

> "'For I know the plans I have for you,' says the Lord, 'plans to prosper you and not to harm you, plans to give you hope and a future.'" (Jeremiah 29:11)

Out of love, in the light of a defining moment, the Holy Spirit will convict us to change. What *is* to be feared is the day we are no longer convicted, for that is the day that the Lord has turned us over to the hardness of our own hearts. But know, in all of this, our God is a God of second chances!

Defining Moments & Deficiency

Along with the revelation of some aspect of God's character, defining moments will frequently make us aware of our insufficiency. I remember the feelings that I (John) had after the answered prayer in Kazakhstan. I was overcome by a sense of insufficiency. Thoughts of "How can I pray like that?" and "How do I get the faith to believe as they did?" flooded my mind. There was never a sense of guilt, for that is of the enemy, but I did feel the conviction to move forward with my new understanding of God. I could not go back to being the person that I was or doing the things the way I did before that time. The challenge was that I did not understand how I could use the new insight into God.

Then God reminded me that He is my sufficiency. I do not have to figure out how to make use of the knowledge I have. God will show me what to do with it. God will show me how to use it. And most of all, God will give me the power to accomplish what He wants me to do with it. In the words of St. Paul, "(His) power is made perfect in (my) weakness."

Discovering your insufficiency may even be the object of your defining moment. God often brings us to the point where we have nothing more to offer, and we are at His mercy. The truth is, our self-sufficiency is an illusion. We have no true understanding of the future, merely an "educated guess," which may or may not be true. Therefore, we have a limited ability to change our future. God may use the skills and talents He has given us in fulfilling His purpose for us, but even the most gifted of us will fail if we trust only in ourselves and what we can see. This is true even of the small tasks, but God is calling us toward much bigger things.

Your second chance is a place you *didn't* get to by yourself. In fact, second chances are designed to take us to places that we *can't* get to by ourselves. They are designed to take us to places that only God, through our submission to Him, can get us to.

The greatest revelation we can receive in a defining moment is that God is our sufficiency. "*My power is made perfect in your weakness.*" Again, we don't know what we don't know." We find ourselves comfortable in our current circumstances – even if they leave us unfulfilled – because we do not understand how much more is out there for us to experience and accomplish through God's power. As a matter of fact, we start to believe that there is safety in the familiar. But defining moments are a part of God's design to pull back the curtain to all of the possibilities.

It is when the curtain is pulled back that we see the potential for what God can and will do through us. It is at this point, when God reveals another aspect of His character and we are ready to surrender ourselves to God, that He is able to unleash the fullness of His sufficiency. It may be at a time when we have been emptied of ourselves that we are finally ready to receive this truth. When you come to the realization that God is all you have, you also come to the realization that God is all you need. When we place our lives, our present, and our future in His very capable hands, we give Him permission to direct and guide us into new opportunities.

Defining Moments & the Identity of God

More than just understanding the character of God, defining moments enable us to better fathom who God is. Since God is infinite by His very being, it will never be within the grasp of finite people with finite minds to comprehend everything about God. The truth is that, at best, we will only be able to grasp small amounts of the identity of God. He has already factored that into His relationship with us. He reveals to us what we need to know about Him, when we need to know it.

How does God teach us about who He is? One way is by revealing His names to us. His name is not a tag put on Him so we might get His attention by calling it. His Names describe Him, and He is defined by His Names. But since God is infinite, even His Names are left open-ended – there is nothing spoken or thought that can fully describe or comprehend Him. He has chosen these names for Himself. They not only define Him, they carry the power of the attributes they ascribe to Him. One of His commandments even warns us not to use His name in vain. In the same way that we might warn someone today not to carelessly handle a loaded gun, we have been warned about the danger of mishandling the gift of God's Name and the power that it wields.

The first reference we have in the Bible to anyone questioning who God is and what He is called occurs in Exodus. Moses was standing before the Lord on the slopes of Mount Sinai. The Lord told him to return to Egypt to demand the release of the Israelites from slavery. The Lord promised Moses that he would go with God's full power and authority and he would be effective. When Moses asked for a name by whose authority he would be acting, God's response was, "I AM. Tell them I AM has sent you." The Hebrew for this Name has three consonants in it and we do not know for certain what the vowels were (there are two common pronunciations in English: Yahweh and Jehovah). Realizing the power in His Name and considering the warning regarding the misuse of it, it is believed that the Israelites deliberately make the name unpronounceable, in order to prevent the inadvertent misuse of the Lord's Name.

> Defining moments are a part of God's design to pull back the curtain to all of the possibilities.

The Name Yahweh is an open-ended statement: I AM. He is everything we need, and so much more. And that is just the beginning of His Name. Throughout Scripture and time, we continue to see God reveal elements of His Name to His people so that they would have the courage, power, and faith to fulfill the purpose for which He called them. In a defining moment, God may reveal a part of His Name in order to bestow a facet of His character we never experienced before, a gift designed to grow our faith, deepen our trust, broaden our belief system, and anchor us into Him. When we have lack in our lives, we can learn of His character. This increases our hope for our future and increases our assurance in Him as our Provider, our Healer, our Banner....

A defining moment is more than simply reading about His Names in a book so that you have "head" knowledge of them. It is where we "experience" an aspect of God and thereby develop a relationship with this part of God that reaches all of the way down to our very soul and spirit. It changes us. A relationship is the only way to unleash the power of His Name. It may be a Name that we have seen a hundred times in His Word, but this time it is different. This time see things regarding this aspect of God that we never noticed before.

What name do you recognize as your Savior? Below is a list of some, not all, of the Names that the Bible reveals to us about God. Please understand that this list is not exhaustive, but it may help you put a name to the character of God that He may have revealed to you in a past defining moment or that He will reveal in the future.

His names are a gift for us to use. They are to encourage us and strengthen us. His name can be a game changer in any circumstance if we have a relationship with God on that level. Use them in prayer and ministry and know that things change when God's name is invoked.

Yahweh (Jehovah) – "to exist, be." – I AM

Elohim – meaning The Lord, the God of Israel, a reference to God's power and might

Adonai – Like Elohim, a plural of majesty; Master, Owner: stresses man's relationship to God as his master, authority, and provider.

Jehovah Maccaddeshem – The Lord thy Sanctifier

Jehovah Rohi (Ro'i) – The Lord my Shepherd

Jehovah Shammah – The Lord who is Present

Jehovah Rapha – The Lord our Healer

Jehovah Tsidkenu – The Lord our Righteousness

Jehovah Jireh – The Lord will Provide

Jehovah Nissi – The Lord our Banner

Jehovah Shalom – The Lord is Peace

Jehovah Sabbaoth – The Lord of Hosts

Jehovah Gmolah – The God of Recompense

El Elyon – The Most High God

El Roi – The Strong One Who Sees

El Shaddai – The God of the Mountains or God Almighty

El Olam – The Everlasting God

These are not all of the Names of God, but just some of the ones mentioned in the Bible. While these are here to give you insights to help you pray and ask for guidance, the biggest reason for sharing them with you is this: Many revelations about God in defining moments are tied to these Names. They identify His character and, through a defining moment, this is where His character connects with our spirit, where Logos (the word/knowledge) becomes Ramos (living/relational).

Defining Moments & Passion

Having seen God in this way, after we experience a defining moment, we cannot be silent. We are compelled to share our victories, our miracles, our revelations. It is a story and a moment that cannot be contained. Like the woman at the well and Saul, the impact of this encounter fills us up to the place where we cannot keep it inside. The urge to tell others is almost overwhelming.

It is more than just an urge to tell what happened, it is a passion. Telling a story is simply communicating knowledge, but sharing a passion is bringing it to life. All of us have taken classes where teachers/professors shared facts because that was their job. You can learn things, but most of us simply remember how boring the class was. If your instructor was passionate about history, though, you felt as though you were there. Their passion made you feel a part of the story.

The passion that a defining moment brings drives us in the same way. We have experienced God's character and we are inspired to help others experience what we have seen. In the same way as the woman at the well, that kind of passions sparks curiosity in others. Her passion prompted the people of the village to come see who this man was. It didn't create faith, but it did draw people who wanted to know why she was so passionate. Once there, they encountered Jesus personally, and that is where faith came into being for them. This is the concept of Peter's encouragement:

> "But in your hearts revere Christ as Lord. Always be prepared to give an answer to everyone who asks you to give the reason for the hope that you have. But do this with gentleness and respect…" (1 Peter 3:15)

Your Defining Moment

Have you had a defining moment? If so, what has happened since then? Have financial crises skewed your view of life or hindered your dreams? Has divorce or the loss of a loved one, a career, or health shifted your focus away from your hope and passion for the future? Have you missed opportunities to dream beyond your circumstances? Have you been so busy that you have forgotten to believe like a child?

> "Truly I tell you, unless you change and become like little children, you will never enter the kingdom of heaven." (Matthew 18:3)

Remember, it is important to understand that a moment with God does not have to be dramatic to be defining. Jesus meets us where we are. Defining moments enable us to better grasp who God is and all the possibilities He holds for us. God orchestrates our future plans when we turn our lives over to Him. Look to God who gives us Defining Moments and defines our moments every day!

For Discussion/Reflection:

- Have you had a Defining Moment? If so, what was it?
- What was the greatest obstacle in your life that you needed to overcome through your Defining Moment?
- What did your Defining Moment teach you about God?
- What do you think your Defining Moment is opening the door for?

Prayer to Understand Your Opportunities

Heavenly Father, forgive me for my independent spirit which causes me to be self-reliant. Help me to understand Your love for me and how you desire good for me in all things. Empower me, by Your Holy Spirit, to trust You and to see my need for You. May I press into you and experience the fullness of Your grace for me. In Jesus' name, Amen.

CHAPTER SIX

THE FEAR FACTOR

The fact that we are given second chances does not mean they will be easier for us. Yes, we may have gained some wisdom through our lost first, but we will have to deal with something else: FEAR. Consider the child who climbs fearlessly on the monkey bars at the playground, taking all kinds of risks to the horror of his mother. Let him fall and get a bump on his head, and he may not be so quick to do the same thing again. Why? Fear.

Like the little boy on the monkey bars, we know from past experience we can fail, and the consequences of it weigh heavily on us when we face a new challenge. For most of us, there is a degree of fear inherent in each challenge, but there is significantly more for challenges we have failed at before. That fear tends to be as strong as our memory of the previous failure is vivid. Time can lessen the impact of failure, but rarely, if ever, will it eliminate it.

Not all fear is bad. A healthy dose of fear is what enables us to live more safely. It may keep us from acting in dangerous or self-destructive ways. It may also keep us alert to people or relationships that would be harmful. In his book *"The Gift of Fear"* Gavin de Becker stated that all of the female victims he interviewed shared one thing in common. They all stated that they felt that something was not right immediately. There was a degree of fear prior to the attack on them. His conclusion was this: if a woman feels something is not right or there is a sense of fear, that feeling is a warning sign and she should stop or take defensive measures. Fear can actually sharpen our senses, if it's kept under control.

The problem with fear is that it is not easily controlled. While there are times that it can be our ally, more often than not it is our adversary. Fear works against us in any effort that involves risk. Fear can be a demoralizer, robbing us of hope. Fear can be a paralyzer, preventing us from taking any action at all. Fear can be an accuser, telling us that we aren't good enough. Fear can be a jailer, imprisoning us behind our mistakes and failures.

In order to embrace your second chance and not undermine it, you must understand and gain control over fear. The first step in overcoming fear is to know your adversary. This will help you better prepare for the attack. Then, you must learn to counter your adversary. This is essential to victory.

Lessons from Moses

It is always good to look to the Scriptures to see what they have to say about any subject. A great story to illustrate the role of fear and the power that God gives us over it is the call of Moses. Standing in the presence of God and His call at the Burning Bush, Moses makes all his fearful excuses. God shows us His response to every one of Moses' – and our – fears.

Moses was born to a Hebrew slave. To save him from the Egyptian Pharaoh's decree to kill all male babies of the Hebrew slaves, his mother hid him in a basket in the Nile River. He was found by a princess who took him in and raised him as her own. He lived as a prince of Egypt until, as an adult, he went to the defense of a Hebrew slave who was being beaten by a taskmaster. Moses took matters into his own hands and killed the taskmaster, but instead of being hailed as a savior to the Hebrews, they called him out for killing the Egyptian. In fear for his life, he fled Egypt and ended up in Midian where he lived in relative obscurity as a shepherd, still stinging from the failure of his "First Loss."

This is where God met him. While Moses was out tending sheep in the area of Mount Sinai, God appeared to him in the form of a burning bush, which burned but was never consumed. God called him to return to Egypt and lead the Children of Israel out. This was Moses' big second chance. But, scarred by the "Failed First," he was not too excited about going back for round two.

In Exodus 3:10-14; 4:1-5; 10-15 is the story of the call of Moses. Instead of looking for an opportunity to go back and free the Israelites, Moses is hiding in Midian tending sheep so as not to call too much attention to himself. Instead of a bold hero stepping forward to assume his calling, we find an exchange between God and a man who is looking for any excuse to get out of his call. To each of God's commissions, Moses has an excuse why he can't do it.

The first thing we learn from Moses is that, after a failed first, there is often a lack of zeal to take a second chance.

> "But Moses said, 'Pardon your servant, Lord. Please send someone else.'" (Exodus 4:13)

As the well-known cliché says, "ignorance is bliss." It is not meant to imply that we are better off because of the lack of knowledge, but that – since we are not aware of the risk – we are not afraid due to our ignorance. Have you noticed how young children will scamper up trees or monkey bars with no fear, whereas those same people as adults will stand four feet back from the railing of a bridge or observation deck? What is the difference? The difference is experience. It is either the personal experience of having fallen and gotten hurt, of seeing someone else fall and get hurt, or worse. While some learned fear is healthy, because we live in a fallen and dangerous world, most fear is the scar of a Lost First.

Moses was afraid after he killed a soldier and fled Egypt. The shedding of blood was an act by Moses; God had not called him to kill the Egyptian as part of his destiny. His attempt failed, and fear took over. He fled in fear for his life, leaving both his Egyptian and Hebrew life behind.

Fear has the same impact on us; it causes us to flee, leaving behind our opportunities for change. You have probably heard the saying "Once bitten, twice shy." Once we know that there is a danger of failure, that there is a chance we could get hurt, we are more likely to live in a defensive mode and less likely to embrace risk.

To the question "Who am I?" God answers "I AM!"

Moses began to make excuses. He did not want to go back to Egypt, and by human (fearful) standards, he had a lot of good reasons. In hindsight, he might have realized they were excuses, but neither he – nor we – see them that way when we are making them. Under the influence of fear, we will see our excuses as logical reasoning. We also learn from Moses' call that God has an answer for every excuse or logical reason that we present.

The second lesson we learn from Moses is that a "lost first" frequently causes us to doubt who we are.

> "So now, go. I am sending you to Pharaoh to bring my people the Israelites out of Egypt. But Moses said to God, 'Who am I that I should go to Pharaoh and bring the Israelites out of Egypt?'" (Exodus 3:10-11)

That is not to say that we have no sense of identity or self-worth, but that we question our ability to function in the area of our second chance.

Moses, who was a prince of Egypt, became a shepherd to maintain a low profile. He had no interest in going back to Egypt or the role of leading the Israelites out of bondage. Surely, he occasionally missed some of the perks of being a prince, but evidently not the responsibility of being a leader and change agent. When God met him on Mount Sinai and called him to return to Egypt, the first thing he said to God was, "Who am I (to go talk to Pharaoh)?" He doubted his own identity and had lost confidence in his ability.

This is an issue for all of us. We question *our ability* to take on a second chance. With doubt, deteriorating self-worth and value, we lose sight of who we are and Whose we are when we listen to fear. But God has an answer to our fear and doubt.

"I will go with you!" That is God's answer to our fear of inadequacy and failure. It is not you who will do it, but God working through you.

One of the biggest reasons for many Lost Firsts is that we did it on our own, without God. Your second chance may be your first opportunity to act with God and under His guidance, as opposed to doing it on your own in your own way. God's Word reminds us of this throughout the generations:

> "I will instruct you and teach you in the way you should go; I will counsel you with my loving eye on you." (Psalm 32:8)

> "My grace is sufficient for you, for my power is made perfect in weakness." (2 Corinthians 12:9)

God's ultimate answer to Moses' fear of inadequacy – and ours – is His Name. To the question "Who am I?" God answers "I AM!" His very name speaks to His sufficiency in the face of our insufficiency. HE IS everything that we need. HE IS everything that we are, for He has made us and given us our skills and resources. HE IS everything that we lack. HE IS more than we can ask for or even imagine. HE IS an infinite God who is revealing Himself to finite people. HE IS the answer to every question we have and every need we experience. HE IS the solution to every problem we face. His name says it all: I AM!

The third lesson learn from Moses' lost first is that fear causes us to question our *effectiveness*.

> "Moses answered, 'What if they do not believe me or listen to me and say, "The LORD did not appear to you"?'" (Exodus 4:1)

I like to refer to this as the YEAH-BUT syndrome. We start out with an acknowledgment that God is capable BUT then we worry that somehow things won't work the way God said they will. What if my second chance ends the way the first chance ended? What if I just don't have what it takes to do the job or to make a difference? What if others don't see me the way that You see me, God?

> Your second chance may be your first opportunity to act with God and under His guidance, as opposed to doing it on your own in your own way.

For Moses it was, "Ok, You, Yahweh, are sending me, BUT what if nobody listens to me?" Moses lost his title when he fled Egypt. Along with the title, he seemed to lose his identity. Could he wield the same power without his title? Doubt, the enemy of our souls, wants nothing more than to strip us of our confidence in who God has called us to be, and thus strip us of our effectiveness. If the enemy cannot remove us, then he will paralyze us. Whatever confidence Moses possessed when he killed the Egyptian absolutely vanished with his lost first. Like Moses, we live in the shadow of our previous failures. *Once bitten, twice shy.*

But God has an answer to our doubts and fears. When Moses spoke of his doubts about the people's reaction to him, God replied with a sign. The staff he was holding became a snake when he threw it on the ground. It returned to a staff when he picked it up again. What He was saying to Moses was, "Don't concern yourself with how they will react. I will be the one who stirs their hearts to listen to what you say."

In the same way, the Lord promises to be with us when we are facing the new opportunities that He has placed before us. He continues to give us signs of His faithfulness today. He reveals Himself to us in His Word and by the evidence of what he has done for us throughout our lives.

This leads us to the fourth impact of fear that we see in Moses' lost first. Fear caused him to doubt his abilities.

> "Moses said to the Lord, 'Pardon your servant, Lord. I have never been eloquent, neither in the past nor since you have spoken to your servant. I am slow of speech and tongue.'" (Exodus 4:10)

Fear causes us to lose confidence that we even can take on a second chance. Moses started to focus on all of his shortcomings. He couldn't have had much confidence as a shepherd; he was out of his element. He had no training when he first entered the wilderness. His life as a prince wouldn't have translated too well. There would probably have been a great deal of humility in transitioning from Prince of Egypt to shepherd of Midian, and even more humility involved in being willing to shape his abilities to manage sheep instead of people. By the time God called him, fear had robbed Moses of a great deal of confidence in who he was. Did he have what it would take to stand in the presence of the Pharaoh? The prospect wouldn't have been intimidating back when he was Prince ... but now?

When we lose confidence, we may use our apparent shortcomings as excuses to not have to move forward into our second chances. The real problem wasn't that Moses stuttered; if he had wanted to go, he would have asked for help with that or looked for another way to do the task. Moreover, when he finally did go to Egypt, the Bible never mentions Aaron as doing the talking, but rather that Moses spoke on his own. The truth is, he did not want to go because he was afraid, and he used every excuse he could think of to get out of it. Fear will do that. Fear will inspire us to look for anything that can justify our unwillingness to risk another chance.

Although our fear prompts us to say, "I cannot..." God's answer is always "...but I can!"

> "The Lord said to him, 'Who gave human beings their mouths? Who makes them deaf or mute? Who gives them sight or makes them blind? Is it not I, the Lord? Now go; I will help you speak and will teach you what to say.'" (Exodus 4:11-12)

God does not expect us to "make things happen." If he has given us the opportunity, then He will also give us the power to fulfill it. This is where pride and fear team up to tell us that *we* are responsible for this chance and *we don't have the ability to make it happen*. But true freedom in Christ Jesus means WE don't have to, because GOD can and will work through us to fulfill what He has called us to do. It is only when we create our own opportunities, apart from God, that we alone must bear the burden of the outcome. Wherever God guides, He provides.

> "For God has not given us a spirit of fear, but of power and of love and of a sound mind." (2 Timothy 1:7 NKJV)

The Influence of Fear

Fear is the single greatest influence in our lives. I know that is a very bold statement, but I believe it to be true. As a Christian, it may be more pious to say that God is the greatest influence in our lives, but the truth is more likely that fear is the greatest influence. More decisions are made based upon fear than any other influencer. It is more than just "an" influencer; it is "the" most prolific influencer in our lives. From our human perspective, it is our self-defense mechanism. While there is no doubt that fear is an invaluable instinct when it comes to alerting us to dangerous situations, it is also a monumental hindrance when it comes facing second chances (and many first chances).

We do not make decisions in a vacuum. There are always influences in our lives. We need to understand what these influences are. We will be influenced by our likes and dislikes. We can be influenced by our perceived ability to do things. We can even be influenced by our mood at the time the decision is made. But none of these influences wields the power of fear. Fear can, and most often does, override our likes, abilities, and moods.

This is why the Bible spends so much time trying to overcome fear by encouraging us to "fear not." The New American Standard Bible includes the phrase "do not fear" 57 times and "do not be afraid" 46 times. Some argue that "fear not" and similar phrases are present 365 times. That is to say that we are told to "fear not" in one form or another at least once a day every day all year long (www.cbn.com). This is the one influence we must constantly be aware of when we face second chances. Only by being aware of our fear can we be ready to deal with it.

Willpower and courage will work for a while, but they will be worn down over time, because fear is relentless. Fear never stops working on us. It affects not only the unknown aspects of our future, but even the known issues of our present and past. Therefore, we cannot rely on willpower or courage to be our defense. The only inexhaustible source of power to overcome fear is Jesus Christ. Jesus, through His Spirit, provides us with the stamina and the strength to overcome our fear. This is why a relationship with the Lord is so critical for our success.

In the Scripture reference above, Paul's letter to the Philippians speaks to this very thing: *"I can do all things through Him who gives me strength."* This promise is not an offer to bring Jesus' power to bear on our agenda, to bless it, and make it happen; this promise is rather a reference to the fact that we are not bound by fear, nor are we hopelessly lost to its power. This is a promise that, in Christ Jesus, we ARE victorious even in the face of fear.

Fear doesn't always manifest itself in the belief that there is no way through this second chance. We may well believe that God can do whatever He calls us to, but many times we think God just can't do it *through us*. This is where we must see that Christ is not our strength so we can achieve OUR agenda. Christ is our strength so that we can fulfill HIS calling on us, regardless of the circumstances we face or the losses we have had. But we must choose to use it.

When we were created, the Bible tells us that God created us to be perfect, in His image. It was not saying that we were created to be "gods" but that God's character was infused in us at creation. We were without sin, and our will and understanding was bound to God's will for us. We did not need to ask God about His will. We knew it instinctively, and there was no place for fear. Evil did exist, but we did not know it, and therefore it did not factor into our thought processes. We knew to avoid it because God had given us that directive.

But God also gave us a choice. By placing the Tree of Knowledge of Good and Evil into the Garden, He was giving us the chance to choose Him or choose against Him. It was not the knowledge of good that we desired from the Tree. It was the knowledge of evil that we would gain. What mankind did not know was that the knowledge of evil was all consuming to us. Once we had that knowledge, we would be separated from the holiness of God and the natural knowledge of good, peace, joy, contentment.

> Fear by itself is just an emotion or feeling. Fear's power is found in how we react to it.

Since the fall of mankind due to sin, the natural influence of God is no longer our default setting. Because of our fallen nature, fear is.

God intervened by sending His Son, Jesus Christ, to "redeem" us (to buy us back) and to "reconcile" us (to make things right again). But we have to make the choice. We can choose Christ. This is God's design for us. It is for this reason that Jesus humbled Himself and took on the form of man, not only to die as the sacrifice for our sins, but also to live victoriously for us.

> "Because he himself suffered when he was tempted, he is able to help those who are being tempted." (Hebrews 2:10)

Christ knows what it is to face fear and doubt, but He also knows how to overcome it. He is here to help us and give us the victory, if we choose to seek Him and His help.

We can choose fear. We can actually choose to embrace fear. And there are many things to be fearful of. Some carry real danger, obvious to any observer. Others seem, to those observing our behavior, to have no rhyme or reason. Sometimes fear has no rhyme or reason to the victim either. But there can be a comfort level with fear. It is a familiar feeling that gives us a false sense of self-preservation. Regardless of how comfortable we are with fear, it deceives us, haunts us, paralyzes us, and causes us to miss out on opportunities created for us. Fear can be the root of anger, pride, rejection and a slew of offshoots completely opposite from the Fruit of the Spirit that grow in a life with Christ.

To make no choice – to do nothing – is actually a choice. I used the illustration previously of life as a canoe on a river that is flowing toward a waterfall. The fourth choice was to do nothing out of indecision and fear, which would result in the canoe going over the falls. The indecision is a choice, and the choice is fear. We must consciously choose to put our confidence in God and trust in His promises.

Fear is not as powerful as God's big three: FAITH, HOPE, & LOVE, but they only work if we choose to use them. Because fear is our default setting, we have to choose to think above the default – we have to choose to keep our eyes heavenward. That is not to say that we ignore reality, but we do not have to view a path through the eyes of the hopeless. We can, through the Lord, be victorious over the obstacles we have in life.

What would you choose to do if you had absolutely no fear of failure? If there were no fear of financial ruin, would you take a chance on your dream job? If you didn't fear rejection, would you try out for that acting or singing role? If you didn't fear losing relationships or reputation, would you leave your family's business responsibility to be a missionary across the country? You may already be in your second chance – but do you really believe you can do it? Can you love again? Can you be financially successful again?

Two Approaches to Fear

Fear by itself is just an emotion or feeling. Fear's power is found in how we react to it. Fear not only influences us negatively; it can also inspire us to act. It calls us to respond. But not all inspiration is good. Therefore, we must look at what our choices are when we face fear. Zig Ziglar, a gifted Christian and business motivational speaker, once shared a famous quote about this choice. He noted that the word "FEAR" is itself an anagram of two possible reactions to the feeling of fear.

The first is **F**ear **E**verything **A**nd **R**un (law and punishment).

Fear can most certainly inspire us to panic and run. In some cases, this is very valuable, but in many cases this reaction is what could cause us to miss a second chance.

The word "fear" has its origin from the Greek word "Phobos" among others. According to Vines Greek New Testament Dictionary:

> Fear, Fearful, Fearfulness [Noun] phobos first had the meaning of "flight," that which is caused by being scared; then, "that which may cause flight,"

This definition suggests that two critical urges will arise with fear. One of these will handicap us and one will compel us to move forward. Often the reaction when we face a challenge – known or unknown – will be the urge to flee. We have the prospect to look at things differently.

Let's consider how we respond to fear. Many of us don't question our feelings about or our responses to triggers in our lives. For years I took the same road to get to work. Every day I travelled the same route, and sometimes I would get to work and couldn't remember driving in. I was so familiar with the road, the route, and the familiar signs along the way that I didn't really have to focus on the direction I was heading. I think my car could have driven itself there on autopilot. When the city decided to widen the road, they made a detour. Many times, I ended up at the intersection out of habit. Not thinking, I would drive to the intersection and have to turn around and go back in another direction. Our minds work in a similar way. We must detour our thinking when we find it leading to fear.

This leads us to Ziglar's second acronym: Face Everything And Rise (faith and trust).

Fear can inspire us to meet our opportunities, challenges, and/or obstacles directly and work to overcome them. In war, it is not always the army with greater numbers that wins the battle, but the army that remains more disciplined and holds its ground. Nothing moves quite like the story of an underdog who perseveres and is victorious. Why? Because we all aspire to do the same thing. And we can – if we are willing to use fear as the inspiration to overcome and embrace our second chances. Within ourselves alone we may find strength to face our fear for a while, but we will never find the strength to persevere to the end without God's grace and Spirit on us.

> "I have told you this so that through me you may have peace. In the world you'll have trouble, but be courageous – I've overcome the world!" (John 16:33 ISV)

The Faces of Fear

Part of knowing how to rise above fear is to see it in all of its forms. Fear does not always manifest as cowering terror. Fear is often subtler than that. Fear will even mask itself as reasonable and logical responses to circumstances. But when we dig down to the root cause of our thought processes or behaviors, we find fear. It can distort our view of things or paralyze us altogether and keep us from moving forward. Consider the following faces of fear:

Self-Protection

Self-protection seems like a reasonable feeling. It would appear as though it was a natural way to protect us from harm, but there are pitfalls. When we protect ourselves, we do more than just preserve our current state. We can shut out opportunity for growth and limit our ability to break free of the bondage of our past or past mistakes. Many things in our lives "own" us: past mistakes, people, opinions, culture, even accomplishments. People do not expect us to change. They assume we will continue to make the same mistakes over and over. Others may *put* us in a box, but we *keep* ourselves there by giving in to fear. Sometimes we are owned by false responsibility. Perhaps you were given the family business to run. Leaving to pursue your dream would threaten family relationships. You'd be ruining the carefully laid out expectations your family put on you.

> Fear is not as powerful as God's big three: Faith, Hope, & Love.

Self-protection is in reality driven by fear. The forms are many, but the bottom line is that it prevents us from taking risks. When we fail to take risks and break free of fear, we are doomed to stay in a safe, well-padded environment. It means that nothing can change, regardless of how much you want it to or realize you need to. Do you have a fear of the failure? Are you avoiding being hurt again? Do you fear success and the position you would hold? Are you so afraid of repeating failure that you are paralyzed?

Failure = Loser

Our culture idolizes winners and so we abhor the idea that we are in some way a "loser." We perceive failure as losing. We will often avoid situations where there is a significant chance of failure for fear that it will further define us as a "Loser." Second chances are especially vulnerable to this because there is, in most cases, a previous situation in which you have failed. The truth is that failure is a part of life. The idea that we can always avoid it is an unrealistic expectation that causes us to equate failure with losing, and we avoid opportunity because no one wants to be a loser.

I love John Maxwell's words, which he used to title his book on learning from loss: "Sometimes you win, and sometimes you learn."

Pain Avoidance

Fear of pain is yet another face of fear. No healthy person likes pain. Pain is itself a warning message to the body that there is something wrong, something we need to treat or protect from further damage. It hurts so that it gets our attention. The fear of pain, especially emotional pain, will often torpedo second chances. In an effort to avoid hurt, we avoid risks, or we give up on opportunities too easily. You don't have to be an athlete to recognize the motto "No pain, no gain." It's catchy, but it would minimize the real value of what is going on in this situation.

The truth is that pain has real value, but we must understand what it is and what it is not. Pain is a warning sign. Pain is not a directive. What I mean is that pain is a valuable indicator that change needs to occur. It is a warning that action needs to be taken – but it does not necessarily dictate what that action should be. In many ways, pain functions like a yellow light at a traffic signal. The yellow light warns the driver that a change is about to happen but does not dictate exactly what the action should be. He can slow down and prepare to stop, if possible; otherwise, he must proceed carefully and quickly through the intersection. In a similar way, pain warns us to prepare for change. Because change is not always pleasant, we would rather not experience it, but when we reach the intersection, we must decide what our action will be: avoid the pain or see it as a sign that an opportunity to grow is at hand.

Scared of Success

Sometimes we can even fear success. I know that this may sound strange to some, but for those who have faced this kind of fear, it is all too real. The problem with success is that, along with it, come responsibilities and expectations. Perhaps we may not have an aversion to achieving our goal, but we do have a fear of maintaining our victory once we get there. We may be afraid that success will expose or make us vulnerable to a personal weakness. An example that comes to mind is from JRR Tolkien's *Lord of the Rings* novel. Aragorn, the heir to the throne, is afraid to accept the position, for fear that he will follow the same corrupt lust for power that his ancestor Isildur did – leaving Middle Earth vulnerable to the return of the evil Sauron.

Once again, we can see fear as a warning sign, but by God's power, we can have the confidence to accept the challenge and overcome our fears and our weaknesses.

Fear can take many forms, and these few were listed for the purpose of helping to make people aware of the need to look at more than feelings (emotions) when determining what is influencing them. Fear may not always provoke blatant anxiety. Sometimes it may seem quite reasonable and logical. The only way to determine that it is fear is by prayerfully seeking God's wisdom and looking at your motives. Many times this also involves the assistance of others, such as trusted Christian mentors, friends, or even professional counselors, to help you see more clearly what is compelling you to act as you do.

Overt & Covert

This section sounds like the title to a CIA thriller, but it is an important part of understanding the nature of fear so that you can be prepared to overcome it. Sometimes the fear that we face is very direct and has a tendency to dominate us into believing that we have no possibility of success. It intimidates us into submission. Other times fear is not only subtle, but it is outright invisible to us in the middle of our circumstances. Like a chameleon, it will blend in to the environment that surrounds it and make you believe that it is wisdom instead of fear.

Overt self-protection can take on many forms. Because they are so blatant, it does not take much effort to see them. Refusing to date or socialize after a reasonable recovery period is one example. For someone who has experienced a failed first relationship or the death of someone close to them, this can be a very real fear and barrier to face. Refusing to "get back into the game" can easily be justified in our minds. We say, "I don't know how to socialize in our changing culture" or "I'm just not ready yet" (even though there is great loneliness or yearning for another relationship). We find ourselves making excuses as to why we cannot try again.

Although I have referenced relationship issues, overt fear can apply to every kind of fear that results from a lost first.

Again, the challenge is not in simply identifying your fears. It is probably painfully obvious to you that you are being controlled by fear. The challenge is to determine whether the fear is justified and reasonable or whether it is part of a self-defense mechanism that is holding you back. Depending on the severity of the fear and the power of its effect on you, you may be able to address it through prayerful self-examination, the counsel of godly mentors and friends, or from a Christian counselor (in the most severe cases). However you face it, the key to overcoming it is to realize that fear does not have to control you. You can control the fear.

Covert self-protection is much harder to address. The biggest reason for this is that you really do not see your actions as fear. What is worse is that you may not even be consciously aware that there is anything influencing you at all. In this situation, you run *the danger of sabotaging your second chances* with no understanding of why you keep failing.

We might consciously desire to pursue a second chance, but without even knowing what we are doing, we may keep killing our opportunities. The result is that we a) don't understand why we keep failing, or b) fatalistically use our failed opportunities as proof that we are doomed to failure with no chance for a future.

By undermining our own efforts, we run the risk of losing the opportunity to live out God's plans for us. We sacrifice our innate desire for adventure and miss out, sitting on the sidelines to lick our wounds. The pain we have suffered is real, but be encouraged – there is more life to live.

As I noted before, not all elements of self-protection are intentional and conscious. For instance, many obese people will actually stay that way and sabotage diets without realizing they are causing it to fail. The real problem may be a fear of love caused by a failed relationship, especially if they have been abused. Others sabotage relationships out of the mere fear of rejection.

I have seen people act in bizarre ways at job interviews because they were afraid of getting the job and failing at it.

Growing up, I (John) was not the most coordinated or gifted athlete. I remember being among the last kids selected to play ball. I lived in fear that I would drop the ball; after all, I had dropped the ball in the past and experienced the taunting of the other kids for my ineptness. I found myself running just a little bit slower than I could or reacting a little bit later than I was able so that I would not be in position to catch the ball. If I didn't get the ball, then I couldn't drop the ball. It wasn't until years later, as a young adult, that I started to push myself to run faster, try harder, and take risks when playing sports. Although I was never "gifted," I became a better athlete than I ever believed I could.

> Fear is a formidable influence, but God's power is greater.

Sometimes a subconscious fear will cause us to act in ways that scare other people off. If we keep people at a distance then they cannot get close enough to hurt us or to see our flaws.

Our subconscious fears undermine our work. We put boobie traps in strategic locations so that, at just the right time, if things are going too well, we can trigger them and cause the work effort to fail. We appear to be trying very hard, but a close examination by people outside the situation points the responsibility back at us. While it may not be our conscious *or* subconscious desire, if we seem to others to be self-destructing, they will lose confidence in us – and may outright avoid us.

Our minds are wonderfully made. They are incredible and fascinating "machines." Our minds can direct our actions in intriguing ways. One of the most interesting is that they can throw up a defense mechanism – even cause amnesia so we/our spirits are protected from what we interpret as critical or dangerous pain. Our minds are so thorough and stealthy about these protective modes that we may not even know why we are acting in a certain way, or why we abhor or fear a particular thing, or why we don't recall an incident that caused real suffering.

In nursing school, while we were studying Psychiatric Nursing, I (Jerri) learned the meaning of Conversion Disorder. The example used to illustrate the disorder was of a man and wife in a boat that somehow overturned at sea. The man could not save both himself and his wife; she was clinging to him and pulling them both down. In order for there to be any chance for either of them to survive, he had to let her go. He watched her drown.

Later, he washed ashore where someone found him unconscious and paralyzed. He spent months in the hospital and a rehabilitation center. There was no explanation for his paralysis. There was also no progression toward health or return of function to his legs; he spent months learning to live with paralysis. Sometime after physical rehabilitation, he was undergoing psychotherapy when the subject of his wife's death was brought up. That conversation led to a discovery. In order to resolve the conflict in his mind of letting his wife drown so that he could save himself, he protected his "self" by becoming paralyzed. You see, if he'd been paralyzed from the trauma of the boat accident, then he COULDN'T have saved his wife. No one would think the worst of him – and he could live with himself.

How complicated, how complex, how convoluted are the effects of fear on the mind and body. The husband could not muster up the strength to walk for months. Physicians performed tests, prescribed medication, recommended passive exercise – none were successful in treating his paralysis. The man himself could not turn the paralysis on or off by choice, but through counseling and the act of forgiving himself, he began to resolve the conflict. He began to move and gain strength, and eventually he walked out of the facility.

So, which is stronger? Is it love or fear? We have laid out a lot of information about the impact of fear, and I think it's important that we remind you that, as powerful as fear is, God's love and grace is more powerful. Fear is a formidable influence, but God's power is greater. As a matter of fact, the Bible tells us that there is no truth to the lie that "fear owns us." Jesus tells us that He has already been victorious.

We only have to be true to our God who designed us and to ourselves. We can be victorious when we trust Him and see ourselves as He sees us.

The Voices of Fear

The last subject I want to talk to you about is the voices behind the fear. Be aware that there are voices that speak to your shortcomings and failures. By understanding who is doing the talking, you'll be better prepared to defend against it. The truth is, you do not have just one enemy talking, but three enemies that will attack you

The devil (The Accuser) is always on the prowl to crush us with his lies. Contrary to popular belief, the devil does not care about us. We are a means to an end. The devil wishes to hurt God, whom he tried to supplant, but failed. Since he has no power to touch God, he comes after us. Since Christ removed our guilt on the cross, we are God's prized creation. Satan wants to steal us away from God, but he is powerless to do that against our will. The only thing he can do is accuse us and get us to believe that the accusations are true.

> "Then I heard a loud voice in heaven say: 'Now have come the salvation and the power and the kingdom of our God, and the authority of his Messiah. For the accuser of our brothers and sisters, who accuses them before our God day and night, has been hurled down.'" (Revelations 12:10)

> "The thief comes only to steal and kill and destroy; I have come that they may have life, and have it to the full." (John 10:10)

Remember, he is a liar and the only thing that he can do is deceive you. Jesus is "The Way, the Truth, and the Light." In Him we have authority over the devil.

The second voice we hear is the World (a culture of comparison). You don't even have to think about this one from a spiritual perspective. From your earliest youth, you understood the concept of peer pressure and the desire to fit in. The marketing companies have been taking advantage of this for years, manipulating us to buy things, value things, and desire whatever they want to sell us. These same voices have been inspiring us to discontentment with *ourselves* so that they can take advantage of us to increase their profits or to give them power.

God sees us as we were made to be.

"Do not love the world or anything in the world. If anyone loves the world, the love of the Father is not in him. For all that is in the world – the desires of the flesh, the desires of the eyes, and the pride of life – is not from the Father but from the world. The world is passing away along with its desires, but whoever does the will of God remains forever. It is a struggle to live in the world and not be 'of' the world. But the world does not have your best interest at heart – and it will be the first to recall your shortcomings and failures in life in order to promote the next one in line." (1 John 2:15-17 NASB)

Once again, the world only has whatever authority we give it. If we listen to the world, then others control us and we will never find peace or satisfaction. If we listen to God, He will give us freedom and victory over the opinions of others.

The third voice is that of your own sinful nature (the enemy within who spies on you and will betray you in a heartbeat). We are more than capable of "selling ourselves out." Many times in my life I have been scared of other people, but the truth is I should fear myself more than others because only I know all of the dirt on me. I am my own worst enemy.

I don't have to depend on another's criticism; I am my own worst critic. I can evaluate and judge others, but I save my harshest judgment for myself. I will all but torture myself with my failings, rehearsing how I mouthed off to someone, acted rudely and impatiently in line, or gossiped about someone. I burn with regret for days. I have allowed things that I have thought or done or said to haunt me for longer than I would like to put in print. Maybe you're like me.

Our enemies will talk to us incessantly. They will rehearse our faults. They will recite our weaknesses. They will remind us of our failures. But God sees us differently. He sees us as we were made to be.

> "For we do not have a high priest who is unable to empathize with our weaknesses, but we have one who has been tempted in every way, just as we are – yet he did not sin. Let us then approach God's throne of grace with confidence, so that we may receive mercy and find grace to help us in our time of need." (Hebrews 4:15-16)

He also intercedes on our behalf, against the lies of the enemy.

> "My dear children, I write this to you so that you will not sin. But if anybody does sin, we have an advocate with the Father – Jesus Christ, the Righteous One. He is the atoning sacrifice for our sins, and not only for ours but also for the sins of the whole world." (1 John 2:1-2)

We are victorious in Christ.

> "As it is written: 'For your sake we face death all day long; we are considered as sheep to be slaughtered.' No, in all these things we are more than conquerors through him who loved us. For I am convinced that neither death nor life, neither angels nor demons, neither the present nor the future, nor any powers, neither height nor depth, nor anything else in all creation, will be able to separate us from

the love of God that is in Christ Jesus our Lord." (Romans 8:36-39)

In order that we don't succumb to fear, we must be aware of it and aware of the lies that accompany it. Our victory depends on correctly placed trust – what we accept as truth and what we realize to be a lie.

Lies are significant obstacles to second chances. A lie is a tool masterfully used by the voices of fear. By understanding how they affect us, we can prevent them from breeding fear and pulling us under. The next chapter will be dedicated to a closer look at lies.

For Discussion/Reflection:
- What fears influence your life and decisions?
- How has that fear affected your view of your future?
- Are you more afraid of failure or success? Why?
- What steps will you take to Face Everything And Rise?

Prayer to Overcome Fear

Heavenly Father, there are many circumstances in life that will provoke fear, but You have said, "fear not." There are many problems that will cause us to be afraid, but You have said, "Take heart. I have overcome the world." Help me to see my fear for what it is and give me the strength to overcome it. Give me courage to see myself as You see me. Empower me to overcome my fears and follow Your lead. In Jesus' name, Amen.

CHAPTER SEVEN

THE GENEALOGY OF A LIE

When considering the name for this chapter on lies, we talked about what we wanted to accomplish. We are obviously going to talk about lies and the effect they have on people, especially as they apply to second chances. This is not about personal ethics or character associated with an individual's struggle to be truthful or honest. That sort of lying undoubtedly affects our lives, including second chances, but we'll leave that issue to be addressed in another venue. We will focus on the lie that is spoken over us and that we believe about ourselves. The lie that shapes our beliefs about who we are and what we are capable of doing. It is frequently so subtle that we do not even recognize its existence.

Our first thought was to label this chapter "The Anatomy of a Lie." It sounded good, but as we talked about the chapter, we realized that this title was too narrow. Even though we will talk about the anatomy of a lie, what it is, and how it works its way into our thinking and decision-making process, that is not all there is to a lie. In fact, in this context, I do not believe that it is even the most important thing to talk about.

To understand the impact of a lie on second chances, we must answer many questions. What is the heritage of the lie, the history behind it? Where did it start (what people or circumstances placed that lie in your life to start with)? How has it become integrated into your life and thinking? How does its history influence your decisions? Like a vine that grows so tightly around its host tree that it is impossible to distinguish between the tree and the vine, lies can grow so closely to other aspects of your life that you cannot tell where the lie ends and truth begins. Like a weed with deep and spreading roots, a lie cannot be killed unless you get all of the roots out with it.

We are going to teach you to search out the genealogy of a lie – your lie. We'll help you understand the importance of going back into the "family tree of your lie" to discover the major events that gave it power and helped it grow, as well as the impact it made on past failures and how it may affect future events. Everyone may not be influenced to the same degree by lies about themselves, but the enemies mentioned in the last chapter will use lies as primary weapons. Therefore, I am fairly confident lying voices try to influence all of us at various times, but especially those of us coming back from a Lost First. We want to help you learn to "break family ties" with these lies and change the outlook for your future. Our goal is to help you discern the voices trying to influence your second chance.

The Genesis of a Lie

If we are going to overcome the effects of lies, we must first start with understanding where a lie comes from. It is important to note that there are two origins or starting points: 1) the introduction of lying to the world, and 2) the introduction of the lie into your life personally.

To understand the "genesis" of the lie, we must go back to creation. Look at the heaven and earth God created. The book of Genesis tells us that, "In the beginning God created the heavens." It goes further to say "...and it was good." As a matter of fact, it was perfect. There was no lie or deceit in the world that God created. So where did lies and deceit come from? Along with our existence, God also gave angels and men the ability to choose Him or that which stands opposed to Him and His values. On the earth, that choice was given a physical form – that of a tree. This tree represented a form of knowledge that would oppose God and His values. We know it as the Tree of the Knowledge of Good and Evil. The instructions associated with it were simple: "Do not eat of the fruit of this tree!"

At some point in the creation process, God also brought into existence the angels in the heavenly realms. Although we do not know how the freedom of choice was represented to them, we are certain that the angels also had a choice. One of those angels, the worship leader of heaven and arguably the most senior of all angels, became filled with pride and exercised his freedom of choice in an effort to become "like God" and be the object of all praise. The Bible tells us that his rebellion against God was quickly and overwhelmingly defeated. He and his followers – one third of the angels – were cast out of heaven to await the final judgment at the end of time. This angel became consumed by his knowledge of evil to the point that there was no longer any ability to speak truth. The Bible identifies him as "Satan," and Jesus himself attached this moniker to him:

> "…the devil, and you want to carry out your father's desires. He was a murderer from the beginning, not holding to the truth, for there is no truth in him. When he lies, he speaks his native language, for he is a liar and the father of lies." (John 8:44)

The intersection of mankind's choice and Satan's influence occurred in the Garden of Eden. Satan would use the ability to choose to entice us to join him in rebellion against God. We do not know if it was a day or a process that occurred over time, but at some point Satan met Adam and Eve at the tree. Here, he preyed upon them and swayed their thinking. He did not do it by simply telling them they should deny God; he did it through lies. Even more subversive, he did it by manipulating the truth.

Satan used the truth that God warned them not to eat of the tree, but he lied about the reason and the result. He made them believe that they could be "like God" if they had the knowledge. He did not tell them, however, that the knowledge would consume them.

Satan took advantage of man's natural curiosity. It was their curiosity about that which was forbidden that put Adam and Eve next to the tree – and within earshot of Satan's beguilement. Added to this was the tempting fruit itself; it looked enticing. They ate it and were immediately thrust into the knowledge of what they had done, aware of evil. And, as with Satan, it consumed them. From then on, lies became as common to man as they were to Satan.

> God does not withhold that which is good for us. If He has forbidden it, there is a real danger in pursuing it.

So, what lessons can we learn from Adam and Eve's fall into sin? First, watch out for the lie that you are missing out on something good by trusting God. The old adage that "the grass is always greener on the other side" applies very well to the first temptation. Curiosity about what they were missing brought Adam and Eve close to the tree. That left them vulnerable to the lies of Satan.

> "Now the serpent was more crafty than any of the wild animals the Lord God had made. He said to the woman, 'Did God really say, "You must not eat from any tree in the garden"?'
>
> "The woman said to the serpent, 'We may eat fruit from the trees in the garden, but God did say, "You must not eat fruit from the tree that is in the middle of the garden, and you must not touch it, or you will die."'
>
> "'You will not certainly die,' the serpent said to the woman. 'For God knows that when you eat from it your eyes will be opened, and you will be like God, knowing good and evil.'" (Genesis 3:1-5)

The lie was that God was holding out on them; denying them the chance to gain a level of knowledge that would make them more "god-like." The truth is that God knew the knowledge of evil would dominate us. He forbids it to protect us. God does not withhold that which is good for us. If He has forbidden it, there is a real danger in pursuing it.

The second lesson is found in learning about the lie that we are capable of being sufficient. The belief that we can be "like God" is doomed to fail for us, just as it did for Satan who served in the very presence of God in heaven. As created beings, we are not capable of becoming like our Creator. We are limited in what we can do, and we will always be limited in what we can do. We are insufficient. But the rest of the truth is that we do not *have* to be sufficient. God is our sufficiency; He manages all of creation. Jesus is our sufficiency; He redeems us and covers our sin with His righteousness. The Holy Spirit is our sufficiency; He guides us to find the wisdom and knowledge that will take us to our God-given destination.

The third lesson is to remember that lies often look really good when they are presented to us.

> "When the woman saw that the fruit of the tree was good for food and pleasing to the eye, and also desirable for gaining wisdom, she took some and ate it. She also gave some to her husband, who was with her, and he ate it." (Genesis 3:6)

It is the nature of lies to look appealing. Who would accept a lie that was clearly untrue, seemed doomed to fail, or would obviously inflict great pain and carry devastating consequences for us? We must be careful not to judge the integrity of something by its appearance alone. We should certainly use our God-given ability to mentally play out the choice to its reasonable conclusion; sometimes it will be apparent that there is no good outcome by doing it. But we should always seek discernment from God and the direction of His Word. If something goes against what God says, then it doesn't matter how good it looks. Do not buy into it.

Lastly, we learn that believing a lie affects our relationship with God. Since God himself is truth, then every lie we believe takes us further away from Him. The consequences for Adam and Eve included their loss of innocence, eviction from the Garden, disease and pain, work and toil and failure. The worst consequence of all was separation from God. Because they were no longer pure and perfect, they could not stand in the presence of Holy God or they would be destroyed.

It was only out of God's love for us that He stepped in and rescued us. He would pay the price for our sin and would give us a new choice: trust Him and believe in Jesus as Lord and Savior or stand alone in self-righteousness and perish. This is the truth, our only hope for overcoming the lies of self-sufficiency and independence.

The Anatomy of a Lie

Let's unpack the anatomy of a lie and investigate how the belief system that we adopt concerning the lie gives it power.

So, what is a lie? According to dictionary.com the definition of a "lie" as a noun is:

1. a false statement made with deliberate intent to deceive; an intentional untruth; a falsehood.
    a. Synonyms: prevarication, falsification.
    b. Antonyms: truth.
2. something intended or serving to convey a false impression; imposture:
    a. His flashy car was a lie that deceived no one.
3. an inaccurate or false statement; a falsehood.
4. the charge or accusation of telling a lie:
    a. He flung the lie back at his accusers.

A lie is different than an error or a mistake. A lie is distinguished by motivation. It is the intent to tell something that is known not to be true or accurate. It could also be something told with the intent of giving a false impression. In other words, a lie can have some truth to it, but it is said in such a way that it intentionally leads hearers to believe something that is untrue. I believe that there is a deeper definition of a lie that points to its eternal consequence.

I would like to add to the definition of a lie this concept: A lie is anything that defines us in any way other than how God defines us in His Word. One of the greatest consequences of the introduction of sin into the world was the loss of our natural relationship with our creator. Up until that time we knew who we were because we knew God, and He defined us. When we lost our relationship with God, we lost the natural knowledge of who we were. As a result, everything in life now revolves around the search for who we are.

To decide who we are, we must first identify the standard by which we will be defined. Since, in this world, there is no "one standard" that applies to all things and all people, each of us is left to determine the one we think applies best to us. But is it an accurate standard just because we like it better? If different people are applying different standards, how can anyone's standard be "right?" Thus, the age-old question is born: "What is Truth?"

God is the only constant in the universe and, as the Creator, He is the only one capable of defining truth. This is why God must remain at the center of our attempts to define truth. While many unique qualities separate us one from another, there are some core truths about all of us that help us recognize the lies that contradict them.

> "For we are His workmanship [His own master work, a work of art], created in Christ Jesus [reborn from above – spiritually transformed, renewed, ready to be used] for good works, which God prepared [for us] beforehand [taking paths which He set], so that we would walk in them [living the good life which He prearranged and made ready for us]." (Ephesians 2:10 AMP)

God has defined us through Christ Jesus. We are not an accident or a side-effect of some other event. God made us in the same way that a master artist makes a masterpiece. God was intentional when He created us. We have each been designed for a purpose that we are fully capable of living out successfully. There is no afterthought with God's workmanship. You are the person that God designed you to be in order to fulfill the essential role you have in this life. You may not have matured or developed in all of the skills you'll need to fulfill this purpose, but you nonetheless possess those skills even now. In time, and with experience, you will see what God has made you capable of.

God's promise is that every one of us is of infinite value to Him, worth the life of His Son to buy us back from our sin. Had you been the only one in need of redemption, He would still have made that sacrifice. This Truth must be the standard you use throughout your life to determine what is a lie.

> When we lost our relationship with God, we lost the natural knowledge of who we were. As a result, everything in life now revolves around the search for who we are.

As a human, you will inherently shy away from any path you think – based upon what you believe about yourself – will cause you to fail. The very fact that a belief is a lie means that it has concealed some truth about you, your capabilities, and your purpose. Every lie that you believe, at some point in your life, will shortchange you and cause you to miss or fail at opportunities.

God presents us opportunities based upon His design for our lives and the purpose for which He created us. The fact that a lie contradicts what God says about us means that we are going to recoil from those opportunities because we are convinced by a lie that we will be unsuccessful. The more lies we leave unchecked, the more opportunities we'll miss and the more we'll struggle with who we are and why we exist.

The impact of a lie on our lives is sometimes difficult to discern, because it runs so deep that it masks itself as our own personal values or preferences. For instance, the negative comments of a parent regarding the skills or inclinations of a child can easily cause that child to forever question her ability to do something, regardless of how good she may be by any other standards.

I spoke with a woman who, for most of her life, buried her talent as an artist due to negative comments by her father when she was a child. His criticism of her drawing and constant remarks that she would never be good enough to make a living at it caused her to hide her aptitude and deny her passion. It was only much later in life that she opened up and shared her drawings and love of art. Today, she sells her drawings of animals, and many clients contract with her to do portraits of their pets. The only way to get to the root of the lie planted in her from childhood was for her to see her ability from a new perspective.

Sometimes we are unable to identify the source of a lie that develops within us. It may not be any one person's actions or comments that cause this lie to take root, but rather a series of comments or relationships that shape us into believing something about ourselves that is not true. Because they run so deep, we can mistake them for values or even preferences. For example, if your work ethic is questioned enough, you might take on the tendency of a workaholic to compensate. This self-imposed atonement may prevent you from taking a vacation or even sick leave without extreme anxiety or guilt associated with a feeling that you are somehow "cheating the system." False responsibility and unhealthy boundaries in that area of your life may seem to you to be reasonable; you're just being responsible and loyal. You may even come to believe that all of the responsibilities of the job depend on you exclusively. If your behavior or attitude toward this responsibility is negatively affecting your mental, emotional, or physical health, or your relationship with your spouse or children, then it is probably not a value, but a result of the belief in a lie.

The Genealogy of a Lie
Not all lies are equal. There is no such thing as a good lie, but some seem to have a more devastating effect on a person. Interestingly, it

is most often not the content of the lie that makes it so devastating, but the degree to which a person believes the lie. The power a lie holds over you is in direct correlation to the depth of the roots it has in your life and history. Therefore, understanding the history of the lie has great value. In the same way that you untangle a knot of string or rope by starting at one end, so the best way to untangle the knotted mess that encases a lie is to trace your way back to where it started. We call this process learning the "Genealogy of a Lie."

The trickiest part of dealing with the lies that wreck our lives and derail our second chances is the very fact that we believe them to be true. Recognizing that we believe a lie is essential to getting at the genealogy of it. It is not enough to simply know that a lie exists. All of us know that lies exist about us. It is much harder to accept that we *believe* a lie to be true. It is not a lack of truth that destroys us, but the belief in a lie.

Ignorance – the lack of knowledge or information – is considerably less damaging than false beliefs. Ignorance can be corrected with training or experience, but a belief in a lie is shielded from exposure and change by the very belief that it is true. These ingrained lies are so set in our minds and souls that they become part of our matrix, foundational to our identity.

When we construct our identities with these lies as part of the foundation, they become an integral part of all our thoughts and actions. Our subsequent new ideas, plans, and decisions are formatted and based upon the original lie. Over time, as we grow and connect to more and more life events, we eventually build an entire belief system based on a lie. The result is a commitment to our misconceptions and missed opportunities in life.

Let me explain. When we are young, if we are told by a parent (this can be anyone who holds great value and importance in our little world) that we are slow or stupid, we begin to believe the lie. In some cases, it may be said out of malicious irresponsibility or spite. In other instances, the remark may have been said in passing or out of frustration. Nonetheless, if we hear it enough, it becomes part of what we believe about ourselves. The lie that we are not good enough or that we are stupid shortchanges us when we forfeit the chance to participate in an opportunity or overcome an obstacle. In short, if you believe you are a failure, you probably will be.

The missed opportunities are endless. Perhaps you didn't try out for the spelling bee or history challenge as a child. As a teen, you never tried out for the chess team or sports team because you believed that you weren't good enough, despite evidence to the contrary. Later, you may have believed you weren't good enough to apply for college or for that new position at work. You began to "settle" for your lot in life.

> A lie is anything that defines us in any way other than how God defines us in His Word.

Many relationships also fail as the result of the belief that we are not worthy of them. Your false beliefs about yourself can affect your choice of friends, schools, and careers. And it can destroy your love life. When you are told negative things while you are vulnerable in life, it can corrupt the basis of your worth, esteem, perception, and outlook. Without a positive self-image, your decisions and view of the world become self-defeating.

Let's examine a more stealth-like lie. Let's say that as a young child you see Daddy verbally or physically abuse Mommy. Then Mommy comes back around when the fire of the argument is smoldering and *she* apologizes to *him.* Your mother may doubt herself and even fiercely protect your father. She may say that because he is the breadwinner and carries the weight and burden of financial responsibility, she needs to be understanding and give grace to his behavior. In this scenario, especially if this becomes a pattern, you may interpret this "permissible" domestic violence as normal.

I (Jerri) have an example from my own experience. As a child I always wanted a friend to play with. This must have been an inconvenience to my parents because they were weary of me asking if a friend could come over or if I could go to their house. If I was asked once, I was asked a thousand times, "Why do you always

NEED to have someone to play with? Can't you do anything alone?"

I loved playing with friends. I remember having a beautiful, pink, fully-accessorized and functional play kitchen in our basement, but I didn't like playing alone. The truth is, most children would probably rather have a playmate. However, I grew up thinking that perhaps I *needed* someone to be with me. The implication was that I couldn't be independently happy. Eventually it became an underlying belief.

As an adult, I realize that we were not intended to be "islands," but this lie was so instilled in my belief system that it caused a dependency attitude. Years later, when my marriage of many years dissolved, I was afraid of being alone, paralyzed by the thought that I could not make it in the world by myself.

When I described this belief to my counselor, she simply stated, "Maybe as a child you were just social and liked having friends. There is nothing abnormal about that."

I was stunned. I had never considered that perhaps I simply enjoyed having companionship, and that it was okay. Silly as it sounds, I had developed the idea that not only my desire to have someone with me was abnormal, but that I couldn't do life without the aid and companionship of someone else. In relationships, these are ingredients for a perfect storm – for everyone involved.

Looking back, I can see how this thought life affected my level of courage and belief in myself. Once, when I was just out of elementary school, I was listening to a second cousin who had joined the Peace Corps. She talked about going to other countries to help fight poverty, bringing medicine and education to those in need. It was the first time I had thought about a long-term goal in life. I had a fleeting desire to join the Peace Corps after high school. I also thought briefly about joining the Air Force at one time, but when I began to ponder these ideas, I was confronted with the fear of "doing it alone."

In my case, of course, my father's early death and the result it had on our family complicated matters further, and those opportunities were simply not realistic for me.

However, a time did come to consider outreach in third world countries when one of my children went on her first mission trip with our church. She sent me photos with captions that stirred my heart. Within five months of her return, I found another nurse who was interested in helping with a clinic, and we took my daughter and her friend back down to Nicaragua for the first of many medical mission trips. We set off with four blondes, 15 duffle bags full of medication and supplies, and hearts filled with the desire to make a difference. We met up with another team from California and, over the course of a week, provided small clinics to people in dire need.

Belief systems based on a lie are powerful, but not insurmountable.

Aside from multiple medical mission trips, I was fortunate to be able to travel at separate times with my children, to the Bahamas, Europe, and Japan. In Asia, we stayed with a dear woman who was a friend of a friend. She opened her home and heart after my acceptance of her very generous offer to come visit anytime. While there, we took the Shinkansen to Kyoto to do some sight-seeing. We stayed in a ryokan (a traditional Japanese inn). I hadn't thought this especially gutsy, until a group of three American men started a conversation with us on the train. They were amazed that we traveled alone and said their wives would not have considered taking one of their children to a place so far away without knowledge of the language and land.

I include all this to say I did do some courageous and independent things – and I did them alone. I never saw them as courageous or independent, perhaps because there were times I was very afraid.

Even after years of maturing, having proven that I could do things independently and perhaps even courageously, there was a season following my divorce when I felt very alone, insecure, and incompetent. I was in such a dark place I didn't know if I could reclaim my life. Nobody likes failure, and I felt I had failed miserably. It was through counseling that I began to heal from such a dependent state of mind. I began to see evidence of strength, and with objective assessment, I was able to overcome the lie that I was incapable of functioning in life alone.

Belief systems based on a lie are powerful, but not insurmountable. It was not through personal resolve but by learning who I was in Christ Jesus that I was able to put things into perspective. Believing God and what He says about us can defeat the false beliefs that have hindered us.

The Defeat of a Lie

Overcoming a lie is one of the most difficult things we may ever have to do in order to be able to succeed at a second chance. We have talked about what a lie is and how it can affect us, but now we must look at how we overcome that lie. It is critical to know that you will never overcome a lie on your own. You need help. Without help you won't even know that you are the prisoner of a lie. But where do you turn for help?

First and foremost, we must turn to God. He is our Creator and even more importantly the only unchangeable source of truth. Though He may bring others into our life to reveal His truth to us, we must always recognize that it is in seeking Him that we will find hope and truth. A true relationship with the Lord, through Jesus Christ, is the only way that we will find permanent victory over false belief systems and lies; it is the only way to avoid trading slavery from one lie for the bondage of another lie or legalistic burden.

God has even provided in His Word examples of those who overcame a genealogical lie. The story of David's early life is just such an example. There is much that we can learn from David about overcoming the power of a lie. Moreover, it was a lie with a great deal of genealogy to it. How did David go from being an insignificant youngest brother of eight to the greatest king of Israel?

We can see in the evolution of his story in 1 Samuel 16 & 17 that it wasn't David's belief in himself, but rather his belief in what God would do through him.

The first lie David had to overcome was that he was too young and insignificant to be worthy or effective. Samuel's account of David's call starts with God's rejection of King Saul for spiritual unfaithfulness. As a result, God directs Samuel to go to Bethlehem to the house of Jesse to anoint one of his sons as the next king of Israel. When Samuel arrived, he called the elders of the town and Jesse to purify themselves and join him in making a sacrifice. He further instructed Jesse to bring his sons with him.

At the sacrifice, each of Jesse's sons was brought before Samuel to determine which of them God had chosen to be anointed the next king. When he saw the eldest son was impressive in stature, Samuel believed he must be the chosen one. But God spoke to Samuel and warned him not to rely on outward appearances. One by one, the sons passed by, but none of them was the one God intended to be king. When all the other seven sons had come before Samuel and God had not chosen any of them, Samuel had to ask if there were any more sons.

Samuel discovered that Jesse had not brought all of his sons. David, the youngest, had been left out in the field tending the sheep, the most menial of tasks. He was thought to be too young and insignificant to matter. Jesse dismissed him as the youngest and explained that he was busy doing the dirtiest job in the household. Samuel insisted that they not sit down until he was brought before him. Upon David's arrival, God identified him as the next king of Israel.

David was deemed not worth mentioning by his family. It was not that he was not loved by his father or brothers, just that he wasn't as important due to his age and the pecking order in his family. In this story the Lord reminds us that He looks at the heart when He decides who has value.

David's victory began with his belief in what God had said about him, rather than accepting the future his family status would have relegated him to. In contrast to David, Saul (the king he would replace) just a few years earlier was also chosen by God, but he ran and hid from the call. He did not trust God, nor did he believe in what God had said of him. The difference was startling. With Saul, his unbelief led him to seek the council of witches, which ultimately cause God to withdraw His support of Saul's kingship. David, on the other hand, believed the truth that God spoke over him through Samuel and *"from that day on the Spirit of the Lord came powerfully upon David"* (1 Samuel 16:13b).

Samuel revealed God's call to David and what God knew about him, and David chose to believe it. This would change his perspective for the rest of his life.

Next David had to overcome the opinions of others as to his motives – not based in truth – to stand up for what he knew to be right. During a time of battle between Israel and the Philistines, David's three oldest brothers had

> Trace strong feelings back to their beginning and expose the lie we have built upon.

gone off to fight as part of the Israelite army. David travelled back and forth between the battlefront to serve King Saul and the pastures at home to tend sheep. One day, Jesse asked him to take some food to his brothers at the battle camp. When he arrived, he heard the taunts of the giant Philistine, Goliath, against Israel and God. David spoke out, asking if anyone was going to do anything to silence him. Eliah, David's oldest brother, was jealous of David. He accused David of being "conceited and wicked" and of coming out to just to see people being killed in battle (1 Samuel 17:28).

David chose not to believe the lies spoken of him by his brother. He knew his heart and chose to act on it, rather than on the fear of the lie perpetrated by the jealousy of his brother. His heart is attested to by his words: "Who is this uncircumcised Philistine that he should defy the armies of the living God?" (1 Samuel 17:26). He knew the power of God and trusted Him to do what men would deem impossible. His boldness was reported to Saul. And that brought the opportunity to overcome yet another lie.

David, full of faith in the Lord's promise, boldly offered to take on Goliath. But Saul looked at his appearance and determined he was too inexperienced to fight a battle, and he was far too small to compete against Goliath. David not only refuted the lie that he could not stand up to someone who opposed God, he refused to accept the lie that God was not capable of defeating Goliath, the one who held the army of Israel paralyzed in fear.

We know the rest of the story. David went out to face Goliath with nothing more than the same slingshot he used to protect the sheep he tended. Although he took five stones from the stream, it only took one for him to bring Goliath down.

What was the key to David overcoming the lies spoken over him? David's strength was his faith and trust in the Lord and His promises. It was not David's confidence in himself that gave him his strength; it was David's confidence in God and His promises that made the difference. Because he believed God, he believed in himself too. Look at what he said to his brother:

> "'Now what have I done?' said David. 'Can't I even speak?'" (1 Samuel 17:29)

and what he said to Saul:

> "Your servant has killed both the lion and the bear; this uncircumcised Philistine will be like one of them, because he has defied the armies of the living God. The Lord who rescued me from the paw of the lion and the paw of the bear will rescue me from the hand of this Philistine." (1 Samuel 17:36-37)

and what he said to Goliath:

> "David said to the Philistine, 'You come against me with sword and spear and javelin, but I come against you in the name of the Lord Almighty, the God of the armies of Israel,

whom you have defied. ... All those gathered here will know that it is not by sword or spear that the Lord saves; for the battle is the Lord's, and he will give all of you into our hands.'" (1 Samuel 17:45,47)

Each of these responses attests to the fact that David did not find the answers to the lies in himself. He also did not believe the lie that he was good enough by himself. He believed that God would fight for His people and that he would prevail by being faithful to God's call and purpose, regardless of what others thought or said.

Principles of Prevailing Over a Lie

Exposing a lie in your life is key to freeing you from the prison in which you live. How do you apply the faith that David had to overcome your own lies? It starts with recognizing that the lie exists and understanding its influence over you. Having others in your life who will encourage you is important, but they will have little effect if you do not believe that you are under the influence of a lie. Like a wolf does when he desires to kill a sheep, the enemy would love nothing better than to separate you from others. Once you are isolated, he'll be able to easily hold you captive. But truth can set you free.

It takes a quiet mind, an open heart, and the power of the Holy Spirit to help us explore and expose the false belief system we have built on the top of a lie. I call this process of discovery – uncovering and understanding the *genealogy of a lie*. Think of it as a study of your emotional family tree, tracing your strongest, most powerful emotions back to their origins. Write down your feelings and thoughts as you begin. This will help you retrace backwards in time.

Understand that lies cause powerful feelings such as guilt, shame, rejection, confusion, fear, abandonment, powerlessness, invalidation, helplessness, etc. These feelings are emotions that you will have to deal with and in some cases overcome. These are also markers. If you experience some of these feelings when facing choices or issues in your life, look to see if there is a genealogical lie that is driving them.

Lies can also leave gaping holes in our lives, voids that we seek to fill or compensate for in various ways. We can react to the voids with anger, attempt to fill them with material things, run away and become distant, self-medicate with drugs or alcohol, or try to fill them with sex, power, or food. Again, we can see these as indicators of something deeper; possibly, these behaviors indicate that we are under the influence of a lie. It is important to understand that the effect of this void makes it almost impossible to simply quit these behaviors "cold turkey." Our emotions and spirit will not tolerate a void for long. They cry out to be filled with something, whether good or bad. They will be much more difficult to let go of if there is nothing to replace them.

> It takes a quiet mind, an open heart, and the power of the Holy Spirit to help us explore and expose the false belief system we have built on the top of a lie.

Although pride may tell us that we can simply "will" ourselves past a lie, the fact is that, without the abiding truth of God, you will not be able to determine the difference between truth and lie. Trading a partial truth for another lie gains you absolutely nothing except further entanglement. Dutifully "overcoming" these thoughts, fears, and lies with willpower, staunch self-control, and discipline is like covering up a deep, severely infected wound with a dry bandage.

We must displace our strong feelings. We start by tracing them back to their beginnings and exposing the lies we built our lives on. Once we identify the area that is under the influence of a lie, we must ask the Lord to come and renew our minds. Consider these words of David:

> "Have mercy on me, O God, according to your unfailing love; according to your great compassion blot out my transgressions.

"Wash away all my iniquity and cleanse me from my sin;

"For I know my transgressions, and my sin is always before me.

"Against you, you only, have I sinned and done what is evil in your sight; so you are right in your verdict and justified when you judge.

"Surely, I was sinful at birth, sinful from the time my mother conceived me.

"Yet you desired faithfulness even in the womb; you taught me wisdom in that secret place.

"Cleanse me with hyssop, and I will be clean; wash me, and I will be whiter than snow.

"Let me hear joy and gladness; let the bones you have crushed rejoice.

"Hide your face from my sins and blot out all my iniquity.

"Create in me a pure heart, O God, and renew a steadfast spirit within me.

"Do not cast me from your presence or take your Holy Spirit from me.

"Restore to me the joy of your salvation and grant me a willing spirit, to sustain me." (Psalm 51: 1-12)

After we have examined ourselves, we are in position for God to displace all of the lies with truth. We can displace any anger, resentment, and bitterness by confessing them and asking for God's forgiveness. Additionally, we may need to forgive those who put the lies in place in our lives. We may even need to ask others to forgive us for the anger and resentment we held against them.

Through this process, the Lord fills us with His Truth (He is the Truth). Only when we are empty is there room for Christ to come in and displace the lie with His Truth.

A part of "being filled" with Christ is "staying filled." To do this God has given us His Word, the Bible. To stay filled with Christ means to be in His WORD. Through His Word, we can replace our thoughts with HIS thoughts.

We conclude this chapter with a final, very common lie: the belief that we must accept every opinion of us or every thought that enters our head. To return to the door analogy, we need to test every thought that knocks or rings the doorbell of our mind before admitting it. Do not allow in that which can hurt you.

Position yourself so that God is able to displace all the lies with His truth.

We have come to believe that it is our responsibility to do something about every opinion, or act on every thought in some way. We may feel guilty if we don't submit or at least respond. This too is a lie. If it is not from God, we do not have to accept it. So before addressing every thought or opinion ask yourself this question: Does it line up with God's Word and His promises? Just because we have a thought does not make it true, nor do we have to accept it.

We must be diligent about the process of healing. Take no shortcuts. Read His Word daily, journal, take notes in church, join a small group for accountability and encouragement, and do not forsake the fellowship of other believers. Rebuilding is no easy task, but His reward (freedom) is worth the time and effort. In the process of staying in the Word and staying filled with Christ, consider these promises and truths:

God does not make promises as we do, "I will ... if no circumstances beyond my control arise" or "I will ... unless I need to change my mind." God's promises are made with all knowledge and with full control. If He promises it, it will be done. It is truth!

> "For as many as are the promises of God, in Christ they are
> [all answered] 'Yes.' So through Him we say our 'Amen' to
> the glory of God." (2 Corinthians 1:20 AMP)

We do not have to come up with answers and solutions. God is the
provider of answers and means.

> "So, he said to me, 'This is the word of the LORD to
> Zerubbabel: "Not by might nor by power, but by my Spirit,"
> says the LORD Almighty.'" (Zechariah 4:6)

God does not always speak like thunder. Often times his voice is a
gentle whisper. Learn to hear God's still, small voice amidst the
noise.

> "The Lord said, 'Go out and stand on the mountain in the
> presence of the Lord, for the Lord is about to pass by.'
>
> "Then a great and powerful wind tore the mountains apart
> and shattered the rocks before the Lord, but the Lord was
> not in the wind. After the wind, there was an earthquake,
> but the Lord was not in the earthquake. After the
> earthquake came a fire, but the Lord was not in the fire.
> And after the fire came a gentle whisper. When Elijah
> heard it, he pulled his cloak over his face and went out and
> stood at the mouth of the cave." (1 Kings 19:11-31a)

God is not a God of fear.

> "There is no fear in love; but perfect love casts out fear,
> because fear involves punishment, and the one who fears is
> not perfected in love." (1 John 4:18)

We have been given a spirit of power.

> "For God, has not given us a spirit of timidity, but of power
> and love and discipline." (2 Timothy 1:7)

God does not contradict Himself. Compare what you hear to God's
Word. He will never tell us to do something that contradicts His
Word.

"All Scripture is God-breathed and is useful for instruction, for conviction, for correction, and for training in righteousness, so that the man of God may be complete, fully equipped for every good work...." (2 Timothy 3:16)

God "Convicts" for the purpose of restoring; only the enemy "condemns" us to oppress us. Condemnation is punitive and can leave us hopeless; it is not progressive and forward-moving. Conviction comes out of love, directing or redirecting us to say and do the right thing. Yes, although conviction can be painful, it is for the purpose of setting us on the right course.

"For God, did not send his Son into the world to condemn the world, but to save the world through him." (John 3:17)

God always operates and speaks within the "Law of Love."

"Love does no harm to a neighbor. Therefore, love is the fulfillment of the law." (Romans 13:10)

He speaks the truth in love to build us up. It has been said: "God loves us where we are – but He loves us too much to let us remain there." God does not speak to flatter. He speaks to reveal the best for us, whether it is what we *want* to hear or just what we *need* to hear.

"Instead, speaking the truth in love, we will grow to become in every respect the mature body of him who is the head, that is, Christ." (Ephesians 4:15)

His Word is active and able to search the deepest parts of our being.

"For the word of God is alive and powerful. It is sharper than the sharpest two-edged sword, cutting between soul and spirit, between joint and marrow. It exposes our innermost thoughts and desires." (Hebrews 4:12 TLB)

He calls us to be Holy/separate. We are sanctified by His Spirit and therefore different than the world around us.

"But you are A CHOSEN RACE, A royal PRIESTHOOD, A HOLY NATION, A PEOPLE FOR God's OWN POSSESSION, that you may proclaim the excellencies of Him who has called you out of darkness into His marvelous light." (1 Peter 2:9 NASB)

The Death of a Lie

So now the ball is in your court. What steps are you taking to ensure success? For this to happen, you must be honest with yourself.

Freedom and victory from any lies that have imprisoned you or are controlling you are within your reach. To be able to fully embrace your second chances, this is a critical step to face. It will not be easy, but it is so worth it. The truth will set you free. It will challenge you to see yourself in a new light.

One thing is for certain. If you yield to God and overcome the genealogical lie, you will not be the same person. It is for this reason that our second chances may not look like our lost firsts. Our lost firsts were based on our limited understanding or a limited person. God knows exactly what we are capable of. His opportunities will reflect our potential. But be prepared to step outside of your comfort zone and understand that you may have to "reinvent" yourself!

For Discussion/Reflection:
- Are you listening to a lie?
- Can you identify what it is?
- Have you intentionally and actively healed?
- Have you laid down your pride at the altar?
- Have you let go of your control?
- Have you learned to listen to God?
- Have you accepted that "God Is" so therefore "you can"?

Prayer for Truth to Give You Freedom from Lies

Heavenly Father, I confess that I have allowed lies to govern my life and dictate my decisions regarding my future. I admit that I have believed lies that have been spoken over me, or that I have said them about myself. By Your Spirit, help me to displace these lies in my life. I claim Your promise that You have come to bring truth, and the truth will set me free. Help me to live in freedom every day and boldly face my opportunities, confident of the truth that You are with me always. In Jesus' name, Amen.

CHAPTER EIGHT

THE DA VINCI PRINCIPLE

We live in a day and age of specialization. Our culture has become so overloaded with information that we can no longer deal with the concept of being a generalist. What does that mean? Despite the claims of humanists who suggest that the "Information Age" we live in is proof that we are becoming more god-like, it is becoming more and more apparent that we cannot handle the information that we now have access to. We are no longer comfortable with the concept of being a generalist, one who knows a little bit about a lot of different things. Instead, we are all being pigeon-holed into specialties, where we know a lot about a little.

Specializing does have its advantages. A specialist has the opportunity to know their subject matter intimately, which enables them to be more efficient and also to be better prepared to address problems when they arise. Specialization also enables a person to develop their skills more effectively and even to develop new ways to address the problems associated with their area of expertise. However, it creates the need to depend on others who have different specialties. The only way to complete the whole task is for all of the different pieces to be in place and working well.

The problem with specialization is that it tends to rob people of vision. We become so specialized that we are no longer able to see the big picture. We start to live life on a "need to know" basis. If the subject matter is different from our specialty, we may never know about it or deal with it; we deem it unimportant to us. But who determines what we need to know and what criteria is used to determine it? We can become so specialized that we reach a point where we don't even have enough information to know why we do what we do.

There may be an even greater problem still with specializing: an enemy of specialization is CHANGE. It doesn't matter how progressive and open you are to the concept of change, the fact is that change is still the enemy of specialization. Why? Because change and progress frequently displace the specialist. A job or task that was important enough in the past to warrant you to specialize in it can easily become outdated or automated in the future. Change/progress doesn't care about the individual, only about the "good of the society or company as a whole."

No one is immune. Those that wield the axe of streamlining and progress today often become the ones who are cut tomorrow, when their specialty is no longer needed.

I (John) myself have faced this truth and, for a season, found myself working with others who experienced change and the pitfall of specialization, When the Space Shuttle program ended, thousands of employees were laid off. I worked with many of these people, trying to find them new jobs through the local Workforce Development Center. The sad truth was that they were so specialized that most of their experience was useless in the public sector. Furthermore, many had been so specialized for so long that they couldn't make the mental and emotional shift necessary to adapt to the change.

So, when specialization leaves us in crisis, suffering a lost first, what do we do? The answer is about 600 years old. The European Renaissance marked a time when the world culture moved from the stagnation and failures of the Dark Ages and transitioned ultimately to the modern age in which we live. It was a time when change and adaptability began to flourish. It was a time when people started to realize that they could do more than fill the previous roles they'd relegated themselves to before. No one personifies this better than Leonardo da Vinci. Actually, the term "Renaissance Man" was inspired by da Vinci and describes someone who is adaptable and diverse in their abilities and mindset.

We are all more multi-faceted than we realize. To be prepared for a second chance, it is often critical that we be open to our own diversity. We need to be able to be good at more than just one thing. We need to be able to tap into other aspects of ourselves. This is true not only for career second chances, but also for relationships and dreams. We need to move beyond what we have always thought of as our specialty. We need to be open to what God can do through us. We need to embrace the "Da Vinci Principle."

A Career of Diversity

This chapter is particularly near and dear to my heart. Although I (John) thought I had very specific plans for my life, God has called me to live a career of diversity. When I graduated high school, I left for the University of Florida with the intent of becoming an engineer. God had other ideas. During my second year, God changed my plans. While I was involved in a campus ministry, God called me into pastoral ministry. I completed my undergraduate degree and enrolled in a graduate level seminary program in the Lutheran Church (I had grown up in this denomination). I believed that this would be my entire life's work.

I was 10 years into my ministry and had pastored churches in Alabama and Florida when, once again, God began to move in my life. I remember distinctly sensing that God was preparing to do something significant. I prayed that I would not be on the sidelines; I wanted to be "in the game" when He moved. This started an avalanche of changes in my life, all of which shaped me and prepared me for this season of my life. It started with a mission trip to Kazakhstan, in which I would see God move in ways that I did not believe possible before. This experience changed my perspective on ministry. It also left me at odds with the church culture I was ministering in. I thought my chance to be "in the game" would be to grow the church I was pastoring, but I faced great resistance and decided it would be in everyone's best interest for me to leave and start an independent church.

I thought the new church would be the venue in which God would explode my ministry and let me impact large numbers of people. But starting the church was a slow process, and I became bi-vocational (working outside of the church while pastoring) to be able to pay the bills. Two years into this ministry, it became apparent that it was creating a strain on my marriage and family life, and I closed the church. After that, I thought I was going to be able to move into another ministry opportunity and resume my journey toward being a major player in a movement of the Lord, but, again, this was not the case.

> We are all more multi-faceted than we realize. To be prepared for a second chance, it is often critical that we be open to our own diversity.

I went on to pursue a career in the secular world while waiting for my opportunity to arise. My introduction to the non-church working world was in the "non-profit" sector. God gave me opportunities in the United Way, the Red Cross (during 9/11), a women's victim advocacy and counseling center (where I opened a new office and a domestic violence shelter), and an employment center. Additionally, I worked as a business consultant in human resources and an insurance benefits consultant. What is most notable is how many different opportunities I was given. My role in each one was different from the one before it.

My initial desire was to work and excel at one job, but it did not turn out that way. The U.S. housing market crashed, ushering in one of the most tumultuous times in the history of the country for jobs and employment. I believed each new job would be my opportunity, and each of them was a wonderful experience in some way. Each of them taught me something valuable, but I still grew weary of hearing, "We like your work and we like you, but we have to let you go."

What made matters even worse was that my marriage failed during this time. As a result of all of the changes that had occurred and the hardships we faced, my wife decided she did not want to be married to me anymore. As a result, my view of myself changed. My support structure and my relationships with other people changed as well. People became more uncomfortable around me because they did not want to "pick sides," and they didn't know how to deal with me once the marriage had ended.

Every step of the way I had to learn not only to be flexible, but also to believe in my ability to excel at the new job or in the new relationship. Though not every opportunity went smoothly (nor was it always the best choice), every opportunity was a chance to grow. While I believe that some people's gifts are more diverse than others, I do believe that everyone can be a "renaissance person."

I have learned a great deal about the process of change and the effect that it has on second chances. I learned about what I lost. I learned about what I could do better. I learned what I was looking for in my second chance. The greatest second chance that I received through this process has been my marriage and partnership with my wife, Jerri. Through this change process, I became the man I needed to be. I became the husband God wanted me to be for the woman God intended me to share life with. In the same way, we have both become the people we needed to be to follow God's call and help others make the most of their second chances.

Lessons Learned from Paul's Ministry

When we looked to the Bible for people who had to reinvent themselves, we found one of the best examples in the apostle Paul. Acts chapter 9:1-31 tell of one of the most spectacular reinvention stories. Paul, who was first called Saul, underwent one of the most significant overhauls of anyone in the Bible. His change occurred on a professional and spiritual level. We do not know the full extent to which Saul was reinvented into Paul, but he certainly modeled lifestyle and spiritual change. As with all second chances, his second chance was preceded by a lost first. So, what was it that Saul lost?

Saul had everything going for him from the cultural and professional perspective. Although nothing is said of Saul's parents or heritage, the fact that he was a member of the Pharisees meant that he was a man of position and education. Undoubtedly, he had been successful in business, which had something to do with tent-making. Providing housing for nomadic people and others who would need portable housing would have been a very lucrative business. More than likely, this had been a family trade he'd been taught. It is probable they employed others to do the work for them.

Saul, although a relatively young man, had already garnished the attention and respect of many of the Jewish religious leaders and aristocracy. He had to be educated in the Torah (Jewish religious training using what we now refer to as the first five books of the Bible). For him to be able to go to school, his parents had to be people of means so that he would not have to work in the family business all the time to help the family survive. At the stoning of Stephen (the first Christian martyr), Saul was named as one present in support of the efforts of those who killed Stephen. Although, probably because of his age, he did not actually help with the execution. This event did seem to inspire his passion to stamp out Christianity and lead to his rapid advancement within the Pharisaic sect.

All in all, Saul was in a very good place, by traditional Jewish standards, to have a very successful career and become a very influential and powerful man in the Jewish world. The only problem was that he had built his career and future on a lie and on hypocrisy. Because it opposed to God – as will any legalistic approach to life – it was a house of cards that would collapse into uncertainty and insecurity. Saul did not reach this conclusion on his own. The Lord intervened in his life. On the road to Damascus, Syria to imprison and execute Christ followers, Jesus revealed

Himself to Saul. Saul was about to embark on the most comprehensive reinvention of himself that any man has ever faced.

The first change we make note of is his name change. Contrary to some explanations, Saul did not change his name. He simply changed which of his names he used. Saul was his Jewish name. Paul was his Roman name. This change appears to be related to the task he had and the people he needed to reach.

> "Although I am free in regard to all, I have made myself a slave to all so as to win over as many as possible. To the Jews I became a Jew to win over Jews; to those under the law I became like one under the law – though I myself am not under the law – to win over those under the law. To those outside the law I became like one outside the law. To the weak I became weak to win over the weak. I have become all things to all, to save at least some. All this I do for the sake of the gospel, so that I too may have a share in it." (1 Corinthians 9:19-23)

When speaking to the Jews early in his ministry, he used his Jewish name. When speaking to the Gentiles (non-Jews) later in his ministry, he used his Latin or Roman name. It is important to note that he did not create a new name, but used the names he was given.

God has equipped us with what we need to fulfill His purpose. We do not need to become something that we are not to embrace our second chance. We may however need to develop parts of ourselves that we have not used as much in the past. Saul, according to the research findings of some theologians, spent almost ten years between his conversion and his first mission trip. It was not until Saul had gone on his first mission trip that He began to understand his call to reach the Gentiles and go by the name Paul. We too need to be patient in understanding the purpose for which we have been given a second chance and use the identity God has already given us to be effective in fulfilling that purpose.

The second change was spiritual. Paul went from Jewish Pharisee to Christian Apostle. Being a Pharisee was more than just a set of spiritual beliefs, it was a way of life. He did not make a simple choice one day to have his name entered on the books as a Pharisee. His beliefs were deeply-held historical family convictions. Years of training and mentoring were required to get to this point. Even more, his position did not come from simply being a member of the Pharisees, but by additional years of demonstrating zeal for the implementation of the foundational values of the Pharisees. At the core of his passion was his desire to eliminate anything perceived as contrary or threatening to this belief system among the Jewish people.

To be a Christian apostle meant that he was more than just another believer in Christ. Apostles had met Jesus personally and had been taught the truth of the Gospel by Jesus and His Spirit. As an apostle, Paul was a teacher and intercessor, specifically called by Christ Himself. What we see in Paul's reinvention is God using the misdirected passion of Saul's lost first and reapplying it to Paul's second chance. In the same way, God will use our passions, as well as our identity, to fulfill His purpose in our second chance. We don't need to fear being passionate or having convictions, but we may need to have them redirected by God.

The Parable of the Talents shows us that God doesn't give us more than we have the ability to manage:

> "For it (The Kingdom of God) is just like a man about to go on a journey, who called his own slaves and entrusted his possessions to them. To one he gave five talents, to another, two, and to another, one, each according to his own ability; and he went on his journey." (Matthew 25:14-15)

God has already given us what we will need to fulfill our purpose. He does not ask us to do that which we have not been equipped to do. If you are a passionate person in your lost first, God will still use that passion in the second chance. If you are a calm person, God will use that for your new opportunity. Don't assume that just because an aspect of your character was a key factor in your lost first opportunity, that it has no role in your future opportunities.

The third change was professional. Paul went from being an elite businessman to a per diem tentmaker. He had built a career on that skill and the network that his family had established for the business. Like other prophets and even disciples before him, he chose to leave a lucrative family business to follow the guidance of God. Elisha was a prominent landowner and farmer before he left to follow Elijah. Peter, James, and John all left successful family fishing businesses to follow Jesus. What makes Paul's situation different, as opposed to Peter, James, and John (who never returned to fishing as a career), is that Paul's original career would continue to play a role in his future.

> God has already given us what we will need to fulfill our purpose.

> "After these things, he left Athens and went to Corinth. And he found a Jew named Aquila, a native of Pontus, having recently come from Italy with his wife Priscilla, because Claudius had commanded all the Jews to leave Rome. He came to them, and because he was of the same trade, he stayed with them and they were working, for by trade they were tent-makers." (Acts 18:1-3)

God may use our skills, developed in our early experiences and lost firsts, to play a key role in our future. Paul went from full-time businessman to a per diem tentmaker. He no longer needed to work at his business full-time. His time was dedicated now to missions, ministry, and evangelism. His skill still had a value though, as he used it at times to raise the money necessary to continue his mission work. Sometimes, he depended on the support of believers who participated in his ministry by accepting their financial contributions. Other times he refused, so as not to be perceived by those he was trying to reach as simply "doing it for the money" (see 1 Corinthians 9). The lesson we learn is that your experience is not wasted. God can, and frequently will, use your professional skills to succeed in your second chance and fulfill His purpose.

The last change for Paul was his role. He went from Jewish spiritual leader to Christian evangelist. It is not just that he changed his attitude about who God was, but he also changed his perspective and purpose. As a Pharisee, his leadership would come from a position of dominance and self-righteousness. He would have worked to gain the admiration of other Pharisees by studying the teachings of Moses and other rabbis. His debating skill would earn him position and respect in the community. But this was not what God called Paul to. As a matter of fact, God did not call anyone to this lifestyle.

Paul's call into leadership would make him a servant instead of a master. He was called upon to yield to the Spirit of God instead of his own wisdom. The emphasis was on humility as a sinner instead of pride in false self-righteousness. His call would teach him to live by grace and look at works as only the response of a grateful heart.

So, it is with us. Our reinvention may take us way beyond attitude. Our second chance may require us to change our behavior based upon the new perspective. We may bring our leadership, hospitality, teaching, or other skills with us, but use them in a way that is the exact opposite of the way we previously used our gifts or talents.

Change & Growth

One thing is for certain, change will occur. All the protesting and all the efforts to resist change will be to no avail. So, either we embrace it and seek to be better as a result, or we resist it and miss the opportunity to improve. There is a saying that has been around a long time: Change is inevitable; growth is optional.

This is most certainly the case. While there is nothing we can do to prevent change, what happens as the result of it is, in large part, up to us. Change is an opportunity for a new beginning and a new chance to grow. It is an opportunity to do things differently and to be a better and wiser person. It is an opportunity to be the person you were intended to be and wanted to be. It is an opportunity. But it is not a given.

Growth is a choice! It is a decision that we must make in the face of changing times or circumstances. It is a decision we must make in the wake of a lost first. It is a decision that must be made in the face of a second chance. Although everyone desires to become a better person over time, what is it that holds us back?

It is, once again, fear. Fear of the unknown. Fear of failure. Fear of success. As we have discussed in previous chapters, fear is an adversary that we must choose to overcome. We must embrace the opportunity to grow. When we do, the sky is the limit as to what we can become.

Failure to embrace personal changes can result in negative personality traits. Have you ever known someone who "used to be" nice, but after going through some crisis or trauma became bitter, angry, and unforgiving? Bitterness can be the result of change, if the choice to grow is not made. Many of the people who slip off in this direction have no idea that it's happening. They are hurt and angry, and the emotions they feel are understandable and powerful. They may even believe that they are "working through the problem," but they really aren't. They are not happy with themselves, but they feel as though they are trapped by what has happened. So where does the power come from to overcome negative traits? It comes through Jesus!

> "In this world, you will have trouble. But take heart! I have overcome the world." (John 16:33b)

Jesus overcame for us both the world and our failures. That is the amazing thing about grace. And grace exists because God loves us so much that He wants to give us every opportunity to become the people He has designed us to be. So He wipes the slate clean, and we can grow if we choose to believe Him and His promise.

One thing is certain. Through a lost first you will become a different person. There is no chance of staying the same. Although an improved version of you is an option if you make the choice to grow, it is not the only option. You can elect not to grow and become less of the person that you desired to be. You either adjust and improve or retreat and decline. There is no middle ground. There is no maintaining the status quo once change has begun (as a matter of fact, change never stops, so there is no point in life at which any of us can ever maintain the status quo). It is therefore more than just a choice; it is an attitude and a lifestyle.

> We need to understand that our potential is defined by God.

In the face of change, it is important to note that your identity is directly *affected* by your environment and experiences, but it is not *defined* by your environment or experiences. We are not identified by our failures, by how other people view us, by our careers, or even by our successes. We are defined by God and the potential that He has placed in us.

All too often, we see our lost first and the consequences of that as the reason why we cannot grow … why we have no potential. But the Bible teaches us that *"…all men have sinned and fallen short of the glory of God." Romans 3:23.* None of us can sit on our laurels and believe in what we could become – based on what we have been. Not if we are honest with ourselves. Therefore, we need to understand that our potential is defined by God.

Willingness to embrace your new world and new role can result in growth and success, as well as positive personality trait development. Things we cannot fix – regrettable words we have spoken or actions we have taken that cannot be undone – must be put behind us in order to move on. A part of moving forward in growth is not looking back. Although it is important to learn from our history the things we want to change or the promises God has fulfilled, reliving the past is not an option. By that I mean that we must not continue to hold on to guilt and emotion – familiar places we run to when we face challenges in our second chance. It is only by accepting our new position in life, by surrendering to God, that growth becomes as inevitable as change.

In a Different Light

Are you able to see yourself in a different light? In other words, can you see yourself differently? Begin to realize your potential, despite missed opportunities. Start appreciating yourself as valuable and beautiful, regardless of your imperfections. View yourself as victorious and successful, even though you may have failed in the past. See yourself the way God sees you.

To be able to see yourself in a different light, you must start by addressing the what is spoken into you. The truth is that we are all influenced by the things that people say about us. While we do not have a choice about what people say to us or how they speak about us, we do have a choice of whose voices we listen to or whose words we remember. We must always be wary of being defined by other people.

Are you listening to voices (your own or others) that constantly speak negative things, things that have now defined you and limited your potential? What is your play list that speaks to you and subconsciously influences your beliefs and behaviors? Many voices may come from hurtful situations that continue to replay in your mind: "You're a loser," "You will never amount to anything," "You are not as...." These voices can go all the way back to our childhood. They could be voices of our parents, teachers, relatives, or even bullies who belittled us. They could be the spiteful words of an estranged spouse or former business associate. If you are having doubts about your ability to succeed at your second chance, there may be voices in your memory that are promoting that view.

Sometimes it is our own voice that disparages us when we value ourselves based upon what we perceive success to be, or compare our accomplishments (or lack of them) to those of others, and come up short. If we do not stop listening to these voices, they will undermine everything we attempt to do to truly succeed at a second chance. We must recognize the pattern and dismiss the negative voices in order to establish change.

Evaluate your self-talk, and notice how often you hear your critical inner self speaking. Punch the power button on the voices from the past. Learn to recognize the three enemies who seek to speak criticism and insufficiency into your life: the devil, the world (others/culture), and your own sinful self.

The process of change may start by simply slowing down. It's interesting to note that studies have shown our subconscious mind will make a decision as much as seven seconds before our conscious mind.[1] We can think we have processed and weighed out both sides of a decision and made a rational decision, but our subconscious mind has the ability to seek to protect us from any further trauma and may be processing a decision before we have a chance to think and pray about it. Create a space between the knee-jerk reactions and prayerful consideration. Seek His wisdom and direction for your life.

Establishing a new thought pattern may start by making sure the right people are speaking into our lives. Not everyone has an objective view or our best interest at heart. We need to make sure that the people we are listening to are godly people who have a track record of wisdom, encouragement, and truthfulness governed by love. If the wrong people speak into us, we will be under the influence of their agendas and opinions. We need to protect ourselves by being very deliberate about who we allow to speak into our lives.

Understand, too, that we weigh people's opinions differently. The approval of some people seems to have more of an impact than that of others. This could be troublesome if we happen to desire approval from those with whom we have an unhealthy relationship. Manipulative or abusive people obviously need to be avoided altogether, but we should also be careful of exposure to those who

---

[1] Max-Planck-Gesellschaft. "Decision-making May Be Surprisingly Unconscious Activity." ScienceDaily. ScienceDaily, 15 April 2008. <www.sciencedaily.com/releases/2008/04/080414145705.htm>.

are "just" domineering or those who may not even recognize their attempts to control you.

Know that it is not just who speaks into your life, but what they speak. Be prepared to break any curses spoken over you or by you.

> "The power of the tongue is life and death – those who love to talk will eat what it produces." (Proverbs 18:21 ISV)

Even good people can say bad things. In moments of anger or frustration, people can say all kinds of things they don't mean. They can even speak curses without realizing it. Saying things like "I hope you fail" or "I'll bet your marriage will fail" or "You'll never amount to anything" are all forms of curses. They can and will work against you. This is where Jesus' Spirit becomes so essential. Through His Spirit you have the power to break curses and overcome words that are spoken against you. It is as simple as speaking in prayer, "Lord, You have given us authority over the devil and the dark forces of this world. I claim Your power to break any curses that may have been spoken over me, in the name of Jesus." Christ has already won our victory. We do not have to live under the bondage of curses spoken by others.

> Be alert. The voices of influence during your transition to a second chance can be extremely chaotic and confusing.

The Danger of Majority Rule

It is a myth that because a majority of people agree on something, it is therefore true or best. The concept is that if enough people weigh in on something, they will come to the best conclusion for a course of action. The assumption is that everyone who is weighing in on the decision has given a great deal of thought to the matter, has done their research, and (most important from a Christian perspective) has prayed about it and asked God for guidance. The trouble is that most do not do any of the above.

Most people are not driven by prayer and reason at all; they are driven by emotions. What "feels" good today is what is right for me. To a greater extent, they are driven by fear. "I am scared of what could happen tomorrow, therefore today I…" Emotions are extremely volatile because they can change by the moment. If they are afraid of something now, they vote one way; if someone sways their emotions an hour later, they can vote exactly opposite.

Multiply this by the dozens of people that can speak into your life. The voices of influence during your transition to a second chance can become extremely chaotic and confusing. Lest any of us think that we are immune to majority rule in our lives, let us not forget the concept of "peer pressure" or the fact that retailers throughout the world invest billions of advertising dollars to get you to buy something primarily because everyone else does. We must therefore make certain that as we prepare for our second chance, we are learning to *drink from a different well*.

Your Reservoir of Influence

Your personal reservoir is made up of those individuals with whom you associate, the activities you engage in, and the sources you listen to and take advice from. As with water in a storage tank, the quality of what you store in your reservoir is greatly influenced by the quality of the sources from which you draw.

Do you need to change your reservoir of influence? This is more than a matter of ignoring or erasing what has been said to us; we must consider where we have gone in the past for new ideas and consider whether they will provide real refreshment in the present. Tapping into a different reservoir means that we take steps to be certain that the water of life that is going into us is not filled with the same old contaminants that caused us our first loss. If we continue to go to the same old sources, we will continue to get the same confusion and instability.

Each of us has a producer or director's chair in our lives. Who is sitting in yours? We may still be acting out what someone else produced or directed in our lives when we were young and impressionable. This person may have been functioning from their own skewed vision and limitations. Who are you listening to? Are they life-giving? Are you growing into who you want to be?

What matters is whether God is speaking into your life. God is not subjective. God is unchanging and all-knowing. Therefore, He is able to see us with perfect foresight and see us as He created us to be.

What does God say about you? We have gone to different books of the Bible for some of the many different statements and promises of God that show us our worth to Him, including Ephesians "...*we are God's workmanship, created to do good works...*" and Corinthians "...*Now to each one the manifestation of the Spirit is given for the common good.*"

These truths are critically important and apply to all of us, but what does God say about you personally? It is important that we take time to listen to God and learn to apply His truths to us directly. His promises in His Word cover us in a general sense, but through prayer, personal study, and the counsel of godly people we can get more specific answers ... not just that we are to marry but to whom ... not just that we are to have a job but which one, etc.

It is not that you are not to listen to people. Rather, it is a question of *which* people you are listening to. Are you seeking the counsel of godly people or secular friends? There is a real danger in relying on the counsel of ungodly men.

> "Do not be deceived: 'Bad company corrupts good morals.'"
> (1 Corinthians 15:33)

Who are you listening to now? If your counsel is not with godly people, are you willing to change your influencers? If you are an alcoholic, you cannot continue to socialize with alcoholic friends and expect different results. If you are wrestling with a call on your life, you cannot continue to drink from the well of negative people and naysayers and expect to have the confidence to move out in faith. If they have no walk with the Lord, then they have no ability to confirm or challenge your choices from a godly perspective.

During a season of change and renaissance, there is real danger in drinking from the well of unhealthy people, even if they are Christian. Unhealthy people are those who have major unresolved mental, emotional, or spiritual needs. These are often very needy people who will befriend and attach themselves to anyone who will show an interest in them. Their relationships are not symbiotic (working together for the mutual good), but they are parasitic (sucking life out of any source that will give it.)

It is a question of which people you should listen to.

Another unhealthy person to avoid is the one who is very controlling or who feels the need to fix everything. These are people who enter a relationship with an agenda. This is frequently the result of some unmet need in their own lives, an emotional issue that prohibits them from tolerating an unresolved change or issue in other people's lives. It is not that they want to help the person process change, grief, or healing; it is more that they cannot stand an unresolved issue and therefore push to have it dealt with so that they can move on to the next problem. Since they are actually addressing their issue instead of yours, they will have a very narrow view of life and no real openness to hear from the Lord before offering their counsel to you.

The danger is that, eventually, we become who we bond with. There is nothing wrong with outreach (helping those who are less fortunate than ourselves), but if we have no strong mentors in our circle, then we are depriving ourselves of the godly advice and encouragement that God desires to provide – the living water we need so desperately during this season.

Beware of the influence of negative people during this time of change. Life can be painful and difficult. You need people who will challenge you to grow and encourage you along the way, not people who tear you down.

"Make no friendship with a man given to anger, nor go with a wrathful man, lest you learn his ways and entangle yourself in a snare." (Proverbs 22:24-25)

Surround yourself with godly, positive friends and mentors who can make a favorable impact in your renaissance. These are friends who will speak encouragement to you, but who will also speak the truth in love. They are people who will seek the Lord's guidance before they speak and try to keep their own opinions or agendas out of their counsel.

"A truly good friend will openly correct you. You can trust a friend who corrects you, but kisses from an enemy are nothing but lies." (Proverbs 27:5-7)

"Whoever walks with the wise becomes wise, but the companion of fools will suffer harm." (Proverbs 13:20)

You may need to change the activities you engage in. During a season in my life when I became obsessed with my heart rate, taking my pulse constantly would engage and re-engage fear in my life – thus causing my heart to race. A person recovering from alcoholism cannot become a social drinker without expecting failure. A person who has a spending problem cannot continue to use credit cards without strict spending limits and expect to get and remain debt free. Whatever it is that must change for you to move forward into a second chance, you must be willing to let it go. If you are unable to stop a sequence of repetitive actions/thoughts on your own, then perhaps professional counsel or intervention is needed.

Making the Most of What You Have

The most critical part of redefining yourself, after you have healed from your lost first, is to simply begin with what you have and move forward. So many people stall out while they wait for other things to happen or for the conditions to be just right before they move forward. The reality is that things will never be "perfect" or "ideal," but that doesn't mean that you are not ready. Know that God foreknew what purpose He created you for, and He foreknew what skills and abilities you would need to do it. Though you may not be aware of all of your abilities, you already have what you need to move forward. Over time, through experience, you will strengthen and hone those skills.

Start by evaluating your skills and talents and determining who you were really made to be. It can be fun to examine and discover our skill set and "giftedness." What are you good at? Is there anything you enjoy doing so much that you don't even consider it work? Perhaps you don't know; maybe no one has ever pointed out the things you do well. There are many self-tests available. Begin by doing a Google search. There are also many Spiritual Gifts tests available online. (These tests are not a replacement for spending time in prayer and Bible study, or for finding a godly support group to help you identify your gifts and skills.)

Identifying your talents and skills can be life changing. Go on a treasure hunt. Search out what your dreams, desires, and passions are. Consider this: If salvation alone was God's purpose for you, and your prolonged presence in this world exposes you to danger and hardship, would it not have made sense that God would have removed you from the earth as soon as you accepted Jesus Christ as your Savior? It stands to reason that your continued presence here means that you still have a purpose. There is still something before you that needs to be done. There is still something for you to do that is so important to God that He would keep you here to do it. This is the treasure that you want to search for! Listen to your heart and notice the things that give you energy and make you excited. What things make you feel confident? Your God-given dreams and passions are probably the greatest tools you have to use in your search for relevance and purpose. Often these things will rise to the surface when we talk to godly, encouraging friends and open up about what we feel most passionate about.

I have heard it said, and I believe it to be true, that "Your resources will be found in your gifting, not necessarily in your calling." It is not always your passion that pays the bills but your skills that give you the resources to follow your passion. It was not always Paul's calling as an evangelist that gave him the resources to preach (although his call from God was unquestionable.) It was often his skill as a tentmaker that enabled him to earn the money he need to continue his work. The key was that Paul never let his skill determine his purpose; it was his God-given passion that determined the purpose.

Know that God's provisions do not always come in the form of more money or resources. Sometimes He simply makes what you need more affordable or even makes what you have last longer. Consider the widow mentioned in 2 Kings 4:1-7. She had very little, but her willingness to trust God and follow the direction of Elisha was rewarded by her small jar of oil multiplying into enough oil to settle all of her debts and have enough money to live on. Sometimes your resources are found in God giving you extra provision; other times your provision comes from God making what you have go farther than you ever imagined. Consider the Israelites. They were in the wilderness for 40 years, yet their clothes never wore out and the supply of manna God gave them never stopped. Where God guides, He provides. It will be His strength that carries you. So keep your eyes open to how He decides to provide for you.

> Go on a treasure hunt ... and identify your talents and skills!

Next, separate YOUR calling from anyone else's calling or agenda. The surest way to fail in your calling is to try to walk out someone else's. Know that your calling and purpose are important. Don't assume that you don't have a purpose and adopt someone else's. Also, do not assume that your calling is insignificant and that you should pursue someone else's calling that is more important. You may greatly admire a professional musician or singer, but if you try to live out their calling without the gifting, things will not end up well.

Similarly, there are a lot of people who will, either intentionally or subconsciously, project their mission and objectives on you. In some cases, they assume that if they have a calling from God, everyone else must also have that same vision; therefore, everyone else should be a part of their mission. Others believe that their calling is simply more important than the calling of most, so the others need to forego their own vision and become a part of theirs. This can be a very serious issue if you do not surround yourself with healthy Christian people. Be honest when looking at your desires and keep them untangled from your obligations or the expectations of others.

Next you need to learn to apply your skills and talents to your new reality. How can you use your skill, ability, and experience in your new circumstances? This does not mean that you must develop a new skill, just that you learn to use what you have in a new way. For instance, although I was a full-time pastor in the early part of my career, I needed to develop a new source of revenue to provide for my family while I was starting a new church. I assessed my skills and realized that my teaching, preaching, and evangelizing skills would also apply to financial development and sales. I was able to redirect my skills to take on various roles associated with financial development for non-profits and sales over the rest of my career. I never lost sight of my call or values, but it did require me to look at myself and my skills in a new light. Perhaps you will discover some form of outreach, a career or hobby that is very different from what you have done in the past. You find that it is also fulfilling.

Take steps to develop your skills and talents. Provide opportunities for yourself. Actively look for chances to use your gifts, skills, and passions. Volunteering is one of the best ways for you to do that. Even though your vision or passion may be big, do not be afraid to take baby steps when you start out. It is easy to overlook opportunities because they seem too small or insignificant. To be ready for bigger things, however, this may be exactly where you need to be to hone your skills. Consider this promise of God:

> "Do not despise these small beginnings, for the Lord rejoices to see the work begin." (Zechariah 4:10 NLT)

Carve out time for a learning curve and take small risks in trying new things – perhaps with a new group of people. One step that could advance your skills is to seek coaching from others who can help and encourage you in the specific areas you are trying to develop.

Be teachable. Don't be afraid to accept the guidance of others, regardless of how mature you may be. There is always something to be learned by others who have walked your path ahead of you. Also, do not be derailed by your failures. Understand that they can be a part of the process of gaining success. Keep the soil of your heart tilled so that seeds can take root and begin to grow. In humility, accept responsibility for your own imperfections and shortcomings. Be willing to ask for forgiveness and forgive others as you rebuild your life. Learn from everything. It has been said that experience is a great teacher, and it doesn't always have to be your own experience; learn from the mistakes of others as well as your own.

Use your map. Don't forget that you have a roadmap to life. Your map is the Word of God. The Bible is a map with all the principles, values, and keys needed for navigating your life. Sometimes the Word contains direct answers, and other times it provides you with principles that can be applied to your choices. The Word may also be used as a check and balance to direction that you receive through other people or in your own spirit. In the Bible, God also teaches you about Himself. By understanding Him you are better able to understand your purpose. As He is the same yesterday, today, and tomorrow, the precepts found in His Word do not change to meet the desires of man, but are a constant source of truth. This map is indispensable if you will simply use it.

A ship at anchor cannot be steered. The only way for the rudder on a ship to work is that water must be passing over it as the ship moves forward. Even if the ship is moving in the wrong direction, it can be corrected if it is moving. If it is at anchor, you can spin the wheel as much as you like and the ship will do nothing. We cannot stay stagnant and expect change. Sometimes we must take a risk and just begin to move forward until we see an open door.

It is equally important to know that we serve a God of grace. Consider the parable of the talents in Matthew chapter 25. Jesus lets us know that it is not the risk of loss that God is concerned about, but the lack of taking a risk at all. God is more concerned with us stepping out to do *something* than worried about the possibility that the chance we take might be the wrong one. While we are not to act rashly or without prayerful consideration, God has hold of the wheel and will correct our course if we will just weigh anchor and move out.

Being Real

It is essential that when we make choices that determine who we are and what we are to become, that we do so based upon a HOPE and not a WISH. When we first read about the difference between a hope and a wish, it was like a lightbulb went off for us. It was a change-maker in our thinking. The insightful teaching and description of the difference between a hope and a wish came from Dr. Henry Cloud's book: 9 *Things You Simply Must Do to Succeed in Love and Life.* We highly recommend this book, along with the others that he and his colleague Dr. John Townsend have written. There is a wealth of solid foundational teaching that has been most helpful to us.

To summarize the difference between a wish and a hope, let's define each. A wish is feeling or expressing a strong desire for something that is not easily attainable; or to want something that cannot or probably will not happen. Hope is a feeling of expectation and desire for a certain thing to happen that there is some evidence to suggest is possible or even probable.

A wish is something you desire and want to come true. It is very subjective. You may want it with all your being, but it is completely subjective and comes totally from you. It is one-sided and has no basis in reality. Hope is not subjective. It is based on objective reasons to believe that good things are going to happen, or at least can happen. Hope can be "God-sized." A God-given hope can require greater resources than we know how to fulfill, but it is still aligned with our gifting and experience.

There was a story about a farmer who earnestly prayed to God for guidance in his life. "Lord, give me a sign as to what I should do," he prayed. To his amazement, the clouds moved in such a way as to give the appearance of two letters: "PC." At this the farmer rejoiced. He promptly sold his farm to open a church and serve as its pastor, for he perceived that "PC" meant to "Preach Christ." After several years of struggling with minimal attendance and no means to support himself or his family, he closed the church and went back to farming. Very confused and disappointed, he prayed to God, "Why did the church fail? I did exactly what You asked me to do." To which God replied, "I did not ask you to start a church. You were a farmer, as I gifted you to be. 'PC' was a call to plant corn."

> The more you understand God, the more you understand your own purpose.

A classic, real-life example of people clinging to a wish comes from a class I (Jerri) took in Psychiatric Nursing. Our instructor asked a room full of nursing students how many of them had married alcoholics and were now divorced. Most of the students raised their hands. His point was that many people go into the field of nursing with a desire to help or fix others – sometimes this desire is based more on a wish than an objective hope. They wish to use their gift of compassion and mercy, but it is directed toward people or circumstances where there is no intent or desire to change. It's important to understand that when you are involving other people in the redefinition of yourself, your wishes or talents alone do not determine reality. Change depends on the willingness and character of the other people involved.

On the other hand, college and professional basketball legend Michael Jordan was cut by his high school basketball team because he wasn't good enough. He knew he could do a better job of applying himself. He believed that he had more skill than his effort showed. He invested time and effort to overcome his shortcomings. His belief was rooted in his willingness to work, not just to believe. Still not everybody makes it by just effort; there needs to be some God-given ability to match it. As Christians, we need to yield to His Holy Spirit to seek, evaluate, and be directed. Then we must be "all in" when it comes to commitment.

Weigh out the difference between a wish and a hope regarding your future. Remember, a wish is based on emotions and not any tangible reality. A hope has some reasonable basis to believe that it is attainable. Understanding how to balance a hope without becoming lost in a wish is critical to redefining yourself in a healthy and effective way. With all of this said, there is still one more thing that must happen to redefine yourself for your second chance.

Raise the Anchor

Raise the anchor and set sail. Whatever changes need to occur in your life, you will never be fully complete before the time comes to launch. A lost first frequently causes us to stop, and we must pull up anchor to move forward in life. There will be setbacks even after we have done all we can to prepare for the second chance.

We must be willing to take the risk. As we discussed before, God can adjust your course. Check in with Him daily to get your bearings (sometimes we may need to check in hourly). You may pass many closed doors before you reach the one you are supposed to go through.

Just remember, if you cannot open the door, then the door was not meant for you. While you may be a new person as the result of the first loss, it does not mean that every opportunity is now a second chance.

For Discussion/Reflection:

- What kind of person were you or did you become as the result of your "first chance"? (What was your most dominant character trait?)
- Are you the same person now? What has changed?
- If you know what your second chance is, what kind of person do you need to be in order to be successful at it?
- What skills, abilities, and passions do you have? Do they align with what you believe your second chance requires?

Prayer to Understand Your Opportunities

Heavenly Father, I confess that I tend to see myself from a narrow perspective. I know that I have viewed life with my own selfish agenda in mind. Forgive me, and "...create a right spirit within me." Help me to broaden my view of myself and my purpose in life. Enable me to see the gifts You have given me and embrace the passions You have placed in my spirit. Empower me to be open to be the person You created me to be, and to boldly pursue the purpose You are calling me to. In Jesus' name, Amen.

CHAPTER NINE

THE TROJAN HORSE SYNDROME

One of the most compelling stories with a moral from ancient history or mythology is the story of the Trojan horse, the legend of a battle between the Greeks and the people of an ancient powerful city/state named Troy. The story goes that Paris, a prince of Troy, came to Greece and stole Helen, a woman of great beauty, and took her back to Troy with him. In response, the Greeks sailed an enormous armada of ships filled with soldiers to attack Troy. They waged war for many months with no clear victor, until the battle was deemed a stalemate. The Greeks re-boarded their ships to return home. As a peace offering, they left behind the statue of a giant wooden horse.

The Trojans were so joyous over what they believed to be their victory that they carelessly dragged the horse into the middle of the city and proceeded to celebrate. That evening when everyone was sleeping from their over-indulgence in wine, the true purpose of the horse was revealed. Inside the wooden statue hid a small band of Greek soldiers. While the people slept, they exited the horse and opened the gates of the city. The departure of the ships was all a ruse; they had landed just out of sight, and the Greek army was waiting outside the gate to come in. The rest is history!

The lesson that has been forever taught from the story of the Trojan horse is that we are to be wary of opportunities. Not everything that looks good *is* good. Not every opportunity is a second chance, and not every circumstance is an opportunity. We need to learn the spiritual art of discernment. It is so important to learn the difference between second chances and potentially dangerous false opportunities. We need to learn the difference between other people's agendas and our calling. The goal is to seek God's Spirit of discernment when it comes to life choices. You must develop a plan to assess life choices before you have to make them.

All of us have dreams – unmet needs, wants, and desires. Some dreams have failed us or left us feeling betrayed. Possibly, we have failed our dreams; they may have been smothered by the daily grind of responsibility (warranted or unwarranted). But some dreams may need to be awakened. There is nothing wrong with having dreams, desires, even wishes, but the risk comes when we try to fill a "hole" or need in our lives without waiting on God to provide the best pathway. When we jump ahead of God to satisfy our finite desires, the probable consequences can create unnecessary delays in accomplishing our real purpose.

Simply strategizing your life is a limited approach, because you lack the foresight to know what your full potential is. You can work toward a change in yourself, but you cannot produce change in all things necessary for success. Ultimately you must depend on a power far above your own, especially to stand up to an incoming and familiar tide that continually washes over you, leaving you helpless to take a step toward even your immediate future. You cannot do it, but God can!

Lessons from "the Man of God"

In the Old Testament book of First Kings, there is a story that has perplexed me all of my adult Christian life. It is the story of a prophet of God, for whom we are never given a name. The "Man of God's" prophecy was truly remarkable and powerful. Nevertheless, the Bible does not give us his name. I believe his anonymity is because he is not to be remembered for his mistake. While his mistake is to be a warning to all of us, I believe God was protecting his identity from being associated with his mistake. Any of us can fall victim to the same mistake, and we need to be aware of the consequences of his choices.

So, what is it that the Man of God did? To summarize the story, the prophet was from the southern kingdom of Judah, shortly after the split between Israel and Judah. Jeroboam, the king of the northern tribes, immediately began to incorporate false gods and idols into the worship of the Israelites, and God had a message for him. Apparently, no suitable prophet was found in Israel, so God chose this faithful prophet from Judah to relay His message to King Jeroboam. But there were qualifiers: he was strictly instructed not to eat or drink anything offered to him from anyone in the northern kingdom as long as he was there, and he was instructed to return to Judah by a different route so as not draw attention to himself as he left Israel.

> Listen to what God tells you. You will need to tune out all the other voices speaking to you.

The prophet delivered a powerful prophecy and backed it up with a miracle in the presence of the king. Although the king was not happy with the prophecy or the prophet, he was afraid of him and sought to gain his favor by inviting him to dinner. The prophet, remembering what God had instructed, firmly declined the offer and left. Word of what the prophet had done spread, and an old prophet from the northern kingdom heard of it and sought him out. To entice him to return and fellowship at his home, the older prophet lied and told the Man of God that he received a prophecy from God that he should come and eat with him at his house.

What happens next is what is so unnerving. During the meal, the old man received a real prophecy from God in which he was instructed to tell the Man of God that, because he did not remain faithful to what he was told, he would not make it home. True to the prophecy, he was killed by a lion on the way home (but not eaten). The old prophet buried him there – away from his home, which was considered a disgrace. This is a harsh example, but we can learn a lot from the mistake and its consequences.

First of all, listen to what God tells *you*. You may need to learn to listen to God's voice so you will be able to hear it. You may know how to hear from God, but need to better discern His voice from the other voices speaking to you. In the Biblical example above, the problem was not a shortage of people hearing from God; the problem was that the Man of God was told directly, and he didn't listen. He trusted what he thought God told someone else for him.

All too often, we question our good judgment and understanding, choosing instead to live according to the opinions of everyone else. While it can be good to counsel with other godly people and compare what they say to God's Word in the Bible, we must be careful not to deviate from a direct word that we have heard from God. Even if you aren't confident that you have heard from God, be wary of the opinions of others, especially if they contradict what God has told you in His Word and directly by His Spirit.

You (and only you) can hear in your heart what it is that God is saying. Do not depend on others to hear for you. Be still, clear the list of wrongdoing in your life, ask for forgiveness, forgive others, and make your requests known to God. Read His Word and see what He is saying to your heart.

The second lesson is to test the advice, or directives, given by others. Do not assume that just because a person is a Christian, older or more mature, that their word is gospel. Well-meaning people can very easily be wrong. Don't discount the counsel of godly people out of hand, but test their counsel against what God has spoken to you through His Word.

There is no shortage of opinions from others. Ask a new mother; everyone has an opinion on how to raise a child – even those who have never done so. Does it take a village to raise a child? Is that acceptable? Only if the village is in unison with the core values and beliefs of God.

If someone gives you a directive "from God," test it to see if it lines up with scripture and the teachings from trusted resources. Take into consideration what someone tells you (sometimes we don't see clearly, especially concerning ourselves), but always make sure it lines up with who God is and how He has moved in your life. Remember, the Lord doesn't use confusion; that is a tactic of the enemy.

The third lesson is similar, but more specific: don't deviate from God's *directives*. The problem for the Man of God was that he not only lost sight of his directive, but he abandoned it in favor of someone else's agenda. Even if someone says that they are speaking in the name of the Lord, do not deviate from what you *know* God has told you to do.

Write down what you know of His absolute instructions and don't deviate. It may be tempting to wander off His path when you don't see the destination ahead. We tend to forget what we are striving for, what the final goal is, when we meet obstacles along the way. It is easy to take our eyes off the goal and focus on the little circumstances around us.

> "Be wary – we have an enemy who 'prowls around like a roaring lion, seeking whom to devour.'" (1 Peter 5:8 NASB)

The last lesson is that there will be consequences for choices that violate God's direction. There is no question that the severity of the punishment for the Man of God was great, but I note two things about his punishment: 1) Even though his life was forfeited before he could reach home, God did not withdraw His love or grace for his eternal soul. This is evidenced by the reaction of the old prophet. Secondarily, we do not know the repercussions of the mistake he made. The indiscretion of the Man of God could have, in some way we are not told, undermined the power and force of the prophecy he spoke. His death may have been required in order for the nation of Israel to understand the necessity of obedience to God.

We face consequences of various degrees of severity. The Bible does warn us not to take part in certain things. If we disobey and intentionally delve into them, we will eventually suffer consequences. All consequences are not "punishment." Some are simply the natural result of our behavior.

We walk in His grace, but we are not exempt from the consequences of sin. Some consequences cost us time, some cost us money, some cost us friendships or careers, and sometimes they cost us our earthly lives. We do not need to live in fear – but I daresay we do need to live intentionally. There is beauty, though, in waking to the reminder that His mercies are new every morning.

> "The love of the LORD never ceases, his mercies never come to an end; they are new every morning; great is your faithfulness." (Lamentations 3:22-23)

The Mountain Road Lesson

As we began to work on this chapter of the book, we took a long weekend to get away to the mountains of North Carolina and do some writing. As has often been the case when working on our writing, God used a real-life example to illustrate a point that we need to make. We were staying at a hotel in a valley. One main highway ran through the valley, easy to drive. One afternoon, while driving to the store, I thought it would be fun to take a paved road up into a neighborhood on the side of the mountain to look at the houses. We were not even a quarter of a mile up the side road when it started to climb steeply, with sharp winding turns.

I didn't think it was a big deal at first. We had gone on other mountain roads before. They had climbed for little bit, but then leveled off. This road was beyond what I expected. Someone who lived in the neighborhood had come up behind us in a pickup truck. We could tell they were getting a little impatient. The farther we went, the steeper the incline became. Our car was struggling. At one point, it was so steep that the car slowed to less than ten miles per hour with the gas pedal fully depressed. It was one of the most frightening situations I can ever recall having as a driver. There was no room to turn around on the narrow road. If I didn't have enough power to continue forward, the only option was to go down backwards, which would have been insanely difficult. And, of course, there was the person in the pickup truck right behind me, growing more impatient by the second.

> We do not need to live in fear. Instead, we need to live intentionally.

By God's grace, we came across a driveway that we could use to turn around. As we pulled in, the impatient driver quickly zipped past us and up the mountain. I can remember my heart almost beating out of my chest as we sat there regrouping from the experience. Then it dawned on me: we still had to get back down that same road. I took a deep breath, backed out onto the road, put the car in first gear, and with white knuckles, headed back down to level ground.

It is interesting to note that the road was not impassable. It was built to help people get from the main highway to their homes. People used that road many times daily and, like the person in the pickup truck, probably didn't think twice about the drive. So, what was the difference between the truck driver and us? He belonged there. He lived somewhere up there on the mountain. He knew what the road was like and what it would take to get there; he had a pickup truck. We didn't! We were ill-equipped and had put ourselves in danger. And that wasn't all – we were actually in the way of those who did belong there.

We talked about the experience afterward and came to the realization that this same thing is very true about the opportunities we have after our first loss. There are streets everywhere in life. The map of humanity is huge. Without foreknowledge of the roads that we are to take, it is easy to get in over our heads. We need guidance from one who knows the way, who knows what it takes to get there, and who can equip us for the journey.

The Waiting Room

God's Waiting Room is the place where decisions are made as to whether or not an opportunity is a second chance. It's difficult to be there and more difficult to stay there if need be. Sitting in the waiting room is not a passive activity (waiting is a verb). It is an active participation in a choice. It doesn't mean that we forfeit our desires, but we yield them to God and His timing. Most times we want instant answers, and we jump to fill or refill an empty spot as soon as we detect a loss. None of us like to feel incomplete, unsatisfied; we wrestle with the very idea.

I remember a woman who came to a singles meeting at a church I attended. She had recently filed for divorce and was separated. She shared that, even though she had only left her husband recently, she was very lonely and wanted to get rid of the feeling. Her solution was to quickly go out and get into a relationship with another man. She had no interest in waiting, but determined that her best approach was to treat the symptom without dealing with the cause. She failed to comprehend that "those who do not learn from history are doomed to repeat it."

All of us prefer to be in control of our lives. There is no question that one of the hardest tasks we will ever have in life is to wait. Yet frequently, this is exactly what God calls us to do: *"Be still and know that I am God!"* (Psalm 46:10). It is difficult to be still when something is left unfinished, especially when we are not sure there will be a resolution, or an end to our need.

We must remember that the consequent danger of impatience is great. Even if we do not eliminate our second chance, we may delay the fulfillment of it by getting side-tracked with false opportunities. No one wants to spend any more time than is absolutely necessary in the waiting room, but if we take a false opportunity, we will never find fulfillment or peace, and we'll find ourselves back in the waiting room. Once again, the only way to leave successfully is to ask God for the patience to wait until He presents the best opportunity. As a matter of fact, God has already granted us His Holy Spirit and the promise that one of His characteristics is patience (Galatians 5:22). It is ours as Christ followers. All we have to do is tap into Christ's Spirit within us.

But how do we tell what is a second chance and what is not? Let's review.

Not Every Opportunity Is a Second Chance
The first step to discernment is fully grasping the truth that not every opportunity is a second chance, and not all circumstances are opportunities. So, if not everything is a second chance, how will we recognize them?

Know this: your recovery will not go unchallenged. There are those who benefit from you being trapped in your past failures. The enemy is trying to derail your recovery.

> "The thief (Satan) comes only to steal and kill and destroy; I (Christ) have come that they may have lire, and have it to the full." (John 10:10)

It is important to weigh all the factors that determine the legitimacy of a choice. But God is not the only one talking. The enemy will take every opportunity to confuse and confound God's purpose and plan for you.

There are many voices in addition to those of God and the enemy. There are voices of your past, of guilt, of authority, and of fear. There are voices of present circumstances, of doubt, of obligation, of well-meaning friends (and not so well-meaning friends). Not all choices are black and white. It is not always as obvious as a good choice versus a bad choice; the enemy can confuse us with good versus best. What looks good to us to begin with can turn out to be disastrous. Be careful who you give the microphone to.

Also understand your emotions. Emotions are powerful forces, and they can create false opportunities to meet perceived needs. Emotions have a place in our decision making, but they are based upon perception, not necessarily fact or truth. As such, emotions can be a very unreliable when it comes to determining the legitimacy of an opportunity. For instance, many people, following the failure of their first marriage, believe that the means to recovery is to meet their perceived need for companionship. Because they feel lonely and abandoned, they mistakenly believe that they must immediately fill this need with a new relationship. Because they fail to understand the importance of time alone – time with God – they find themselves dealing with the same problem and outcome again and again.

Those who do not learn from history are doomed to repeat it. And usually the end result is not a good one!

Some false opportunities fall within God's *permissive* will but not His *perfect* will. There are things we can do that God will allow, but they are not what He desires most for us. This is the struggle between good opportunities and best opportunities. Not all false opportunities have devastating results, but they may make us miss opportunities for what is best. We need to be aware that there is always a best opportunity for us, one that God has been preparing us for. The key is to be looking for the best and not settle for something that is good just because it appears first.

Most false opportunities are the result of our ignorance of God's plan. If we do not draw close to God and seek Him and His direction for our lives, we will never understand what it is we are supposed to do. It is critically important that we learn to hear His voice. Spending time with someone allows you to grow close and become familiar with them. So it is with God – the more time we spend with Him, the more in tune with His voice we become and the more discerning we become of His guidance.

The truth of God's vastness resides in this promise: *"Jesus looked at them and said, 'With man this is impossible, but with God all things are possible.'" Matthew 19:26.* He meets us where we are. He uses what we have brought with us. He works through us in spite of our shortcomings and He desires relationship over religious actions.

Second Chance vs. Dangerous Mistake

What is the difference between a second chance and a potentially dangerous opportunity? While it is easy to think that any given opportunity may be our second chance – some prospects have the potential of doing more harm than good. For instance, in the wake of a recent divorce, developing a relationship prior to healing may be disastrous. Part of healing is learning from the "loss." If we do not learn from past failures or crises– our default is to repeat our past because it is familiar. Repeating our mistakes in the light of a new situation can lead to worse consequences than our first loss.

When we have lost something we naturally look to replace it – to fill a need. Two of the most critical needs during this time are patience and guidance. The problem is that we frequently do not take the time or effort to employ either of them. It is of utmost importance that we exercise patience while at the same time pursue guidance to determine the best course of direction following an ending or a loss.

A potentially dangerous opportunity would be one that looks to fill a part of our lives that has been lost without taking the time to see things clearly through the best possible counsel. Sometimes it is a spontaneous action motivated by boredom, loneliness, anger or jealousy. Some opportunities are good but not best, and we choose them because we are weary of waiting on something to open for us. Our impatience only delays God's best for us. The best way to discern the difference between a second chance and a dangerous mistake is to seek God's wisdom.

Ask the following questions. It is essential to know that the answers will only help if you yield to God first and are COMPLETELY HONEST WITH YOURSELF!

Why do I believe that this is the right choice?

Taking the time to evaluate why you make a decision is a good habit to get into. Check your motives. Do you allow life to dictate your decision? Are you riding the flow of circumstances, taking whatever life gives you?

Living decisively will take practice. Devote time to being still and listening to God; it does not come naturally. Most of us want to dictate who we are, who we become, and what we do with opportunities that come our way. If we have made a decision to follow Christ, to proclaim we are God's and follow His plan for our lives, we must learn to yield to Him.

Is this an emotional decision or reasonably thought out?

Emotions are an integral part of human existence, so it is not a matter of whether or not emotions factor into a decision, but to what extent. If we keep this fact in mind, we stand a better chance of keeping our emotions balanced with reasonable thought. While we may need to consider how we feel about a particular option, we must also know that our feeling can change in a matter of minutes and can change many times on the same issue. Therefore, it is important that we look at our options as logically as we can to balance this out.

A good practice to help this happen is to make a list on a sheet of paper listing the pros and cons of each decision. You may need to add to this list over a period of days or weeks depending on the complexity and importance of the decision. Do not try to rush this or you may postpone God's blessing or, worst of all, miss it. Pray for a discerning spirit, then review the facts on your list and weigh them against your emotions. You will find a great deal more peace and confidence with the choices you make.

Is my decision filling a need (temporarily solving a problem) or moving forward toward a goal?

Are you looking backward or are you looking forward? If you do nothing but react to needs, you will never have consistent direction in your life. That is like walking forward while looking in the rearview mirror. I've heard it asked, "Why do you think the front window shield is so large and the rearview mirror so small?" The answer, of course, is that seeing what is in front of us is infinitely more important that concentrating on what is behind us. Only by looking forward can you successfully move on.

> The more you feel the need to justify your decision, especially to yourself and others who have not questioned it, the more likely it is that you are not being truthful about your choice.

Football players, track athletes, and jockeys are all taught something very early on in their training: focus on your goal. Do not look back. Use your peripheral vision to determine your situation, but do not look back. Time and again, athletes have lost races or been tackled short of a touchdown because they turned around to look behind them. By looking back, the athlete not only lost sight of his goal, he lost a step. Turning around physically slowed him down, allowing those who were behind, who were focused forward, to overtake him. So it is with your choices. If you stay focused on your goal, you will achieve far more than if you simply try to fill a need created by past loss.

Am I feeling the need to justify my choice, or am I truly at peace?

The more you feel the need to justify your decision, especially to yourself and others who have not questioned it, the more likely it is that you are not being truthful about your choice. This usually reflects an issue with the motivation for the choice as much as with the choice itself. When you ask these questions, it can be very tempting to succumb to the pressure of others. There is also the temptation to "end the pain" or just "fill the gap" and therefore manipulate the answers to the questions to make this the "right choice."

The good news is that God has placed a safety mechanism within us. That mechanism is your conscience. When you violate a core value, your conscience will not let it go. You will sense a "check" in your spirit which you can neither explain nor escape. It is there to make you aware that something is not right. The evidence your conscience is at work is most often an intense sense that you must justify your decision, especially to yourself. The most dangerous consequence of ignoring those spirit checks is that, eventually, you can suppress your conscience until you do not hear it anymore.

In the end, even if you ignore your conscience and lie to yourself about your choice or the reason for it, that will not change the consequences of an unwise decision. Be honest with yourself and listen to your conscience. You do not always have to learn the hard way or repeat the same mistake over and over. Seek God first, and you'll have peace with your decisions, even when they are difficult.

Is our decision compromising our ethics and morals?

Be alert to situation ethics/morals when making decisions about an opportunity.

> "The way of a fool is right in his own eyes, but a wise man is he who listens to counsel." (Proverbs 12:15)

Does the "end" justify the means? No, it does not! There may be a temptation to excuse behavior such as deception or manipulation to achieve a goal if we believe that the desired result will be in our favor. The price that is paid for this kind of decision is at the expense of our character. If we sacrifice our character, in the end, even achieving our goal will be a bittersweet victory. We may get what we want in the short term, but we could lose friendships and credibility permanently because of it. It is okay to strive for our goals, but we must always maintain our honor and our integrity in the process. God-given patience is the tool that we have to help us be successful and honorable at the same time.

Do I reply to advice I don't like, "Yes, but…"?

There are those who seek counsel BUT always have an excuse or argument for why the advice won't work. This is the sign of an unteachable spirit. No, we do not have to accept everything that people tell us, but we must be willing to honestly give thoughtful consideration to advice from mature godly believers. It is wearying for others when we constantly ask for their advice but never give it any real consideration. This mindset causes those around us to withdraw and stop counseling. We may lose the very source of counsel that God has chosen to speak to us. Listen to those who are godly and whose insight you respect.

Who am I doing this for?

The saying "We often spend money (or time) that we don't have to impress people we don't like who in all likelihood don't care" is relevant and too often true.

It is not uncommon to feel the compulsion to subject ourselves to certain people in our lives. This is especially true for those living in an obligatory manner, answering to others out of indebtedness, (false) guilt, or shame. Some of us allow unhealthy relationships to develop and control us. This is especially an issue for domestic violence victims, but it is not limited to domestic violence.

Any of us can succumb to someone who has exerted inappropriate or unhealthy control over our lives. This can include parents who continue to exercise unhealthy and inappropriate influence over their adult children. Parents have a responsibility to care for and guide their minor children, but it becomes unhealthy when they seek to control the lives of their adult children and interfere with their relationships.

People who seek to influence your decisions are usually doing so as a result of their agenda. You simply become a means to an end for them. Focus on making the decision based upon what God is saying to you and on the resources He is providing you.

Avoid pursuing opportunities to impress or prove something to people you believe are responsible for your first loss. I cannot begin to tell you how many times I have met people whose primary, if not only, motivation for doing something was to prove to someone else that they could do it. Most often that person was someone they credited with their first loss. Any decision with this kind of motivation is doomed to failure. Even good choices made with the wrong motivation will fail, because they will never produce the satisfaction you're looking for.

Avoid pursuing opportunities to prove something to yourself. This is a trap. We build it ourselves. We begin by comparing ourselves and our accomplishments with others in order to determine our own worth and effectiveness. But since there is no one exactly like you, with your exact skill set and your exact personality, no accurate comparison can be made. Your self-worth does not come from what you accomplish, nor do your failures define you. We are unique creations of our Maker. Therefore, only God can define us and give us self-worth.

> "Yes, all have sinned; all fall short of God's glorious ideal; yet now God declares us 'not guilty' of offending him if we trust in Jesus Christ, who in his kindness freely takes away our sins." (Romans 3:23-24 TLB)

He has deemed us worth the life of His Son, Jesus. This is what defines us, not what we do. Let God direct you and He will back it up.

> "The Lord said to me, 'You have seen correctly, for I am watching to see that my word is fulfilled.'" (Jeremiah 1:12)

God has promised to be with us and provide what we need to accomplish His purpose. Time and again throughout the previous chapters we have seen His promises. Seeking Him first and being willing to wait on His direction is key to moving out under His protection. Seeking Him is how we find our second chance and succeed at it.

Does my choice line up with what God teaches in the Bible?

For you to know the answer to this question, you must be in the Word, and we will discuss this more a little later.

Telling the Difference

There are bad decisions, good decisions, better decisions, and best decisions. Making the right choice can be confusing and overwhelming. But it is not a matter of guesswork. You can make an informed decision, but since none of us knows the future, the only way to make an informed decision is to involve the One who knows the future. We must count on God's guidance.

So, how do you know what God's guidance is? First of all, you must be in God's Word. There is no understating the importance of being in God's Word for yourself. The gift of God's Word and His Spirit has been given so that no one would ever have to be at the mercy of others to discern God's plan and will for them. Each of us can go directly into the Word to learn the basic principles of life.

> Even good choices made with the wrong motivation will fail, because they will never produce the satisfaction you're looking for.

When we study math, we are not taught the answer to every individual conceivable numerical problem; we are provided with formulas to apply to determine the answers. God's Word does not address every issue specifically and directly, but it does lay out principles that we must apply to determine the parameters of our choices.

God's Word is unchanging and based upon His perfect design. Although people's opinions may change, you will never find that the Word of God was deficient having not taking into account some truth that will be revealed later. God planned for everything in His Word, but to access it we must read it.

Often the best approach is to simply pick up the Bible and start reading it. You can start from anywhere in the Bible, but the best place may be to start with the New Testament Gospels: the books of Matthew, Mark, Luke, or John. Your local church is a wonderful place to start. There are also many other resources on the internet to help guide you through the Bible.

Other aides may be devotional materials. These accompany Bible reading, but they also speak words of encouragement or admonishment based upon the verses that they use. Commentaries or non-fiction Christian work can also be used as an aide in understanding what God is saying. While these do not replace reading the Bible, they can be a great help in understanding what the Bible says regarding various issues.

But what about your specific situation and choices? If you can't find your answer directly in the Word, how do you determine what God is saying specifically to you?

Start with prayer. Ask for God's Spirit of guidance and for discernment to understand what is best. Then, seek the godly counsel of others. Look at some of the verses in Proverbs that speak to seeking advice and godly counsel:

> "Listen to counsel and accept discipline, that you may be wise the rest of your days." (Proverbs 19:20)

> "A wise man will hear and increase in learning, And a man of understanding will acquire wise counsel." (Proverbs 1:5)

Look for someone who will also seek God's will on your behalf. One who gives quick advice may not give you godly wisdom; they may simply tell you what they think you want to hear. A wise counselor will often ask more questions of you than they will give you answers or opinions. A wise counselor will help you to hear from God, more than just speak God's direction to you.

You may wish to start with a trusted mentor. Is there someone in your life whom you have been able to go to before to help you understand something in God's Word? Do you know someone whose life shows a history of godly, wise counsel? A mentor must necessarily know things about your situation and history before they can speak into your life. Your relationship with this individual will require a high level of trust. Look for someone who has already earned your confidence so that when they speak the truth in love, you will be more inclined to hear it and act on it.

Seek the input of multiple godly people, if possible.

> "Without consultation, plans are frustrated, but with many counselors they succeed." (Proverbs 15:22)

It is not always possible to get the counsel of more than one godly person, but when possible, it is always better. One benefit of having multiple counselors is that it reduces the danger of just getting an opinion, as opposed to true godly counsel. Godly counsel allows for the expression of a dissenting view while still giving you balance in your understanding. It is true that no one knows you like you know yourself, but there are people who may know a lot about a particular aspect of your life and calling. The value of multiple counselors is that different people can help you understand the different aspects of your choice and what God is saying to you in multiple areas of your life.

Invest time in those who will speak the truth to you, and do so in love.

Seek the godly advice of someone who has faced the same choice, regardless of whether they failed or succeeded. You can learn and benefit from both their success and failure. Their experience gives them unique insight into the possibilities and the potential problems you may be facing in your decision. Their situation won't be exactly like yours, but people who have faced lost firsts and found second chances tend to be most sensitive to the uniqueness of another's situation. They will be less dogmatic and more understanding while they share their experiences – good or bad. This is what makes their counsel so valuable.

Look for the inner prompting of the Holy Spirit.

> "But when He, the Spirit of truth, comes, He will guide you into all the truth; for He will not speak on His own

initiative, but whatever He hears, He will speak; and He will disclose to you what is to come." (John 16:13)

Jesus gave us the ability to stay in touch with Him always, just as He promised. It is the gift of the Holy Spirit. The Holy Spirit leads us and guides us through various ways. His is not usually an audible voice, but rather a sense of His guidance that emanates from deep within us. More than a "gut feeling," this is a sense of godly direction, but it comes from a place not easily described. Our ability to distinguish His voice comes with practice, over time. Some are more skilled at hearing the Spirit's promptings, but all can learn and improve. God's Spirit does speak to us and, with Bible study and the counsel of godly people, inner prompting is an essential element in distinguishing a second chance and God's best opportunity for us.

Avoid the counsel of "friends" or other "yes men." More and more, people want to be politically correct; they do not want to offend. Tough love is hard to come by. Good, solid friendships push us to grow in the Lord. Those relationships require time and effort. Invest time in those who will speak the truth to you, and do so in love.

As you move toward your choice, look for clues that you are on the right path, signs that you have made the right choice or that you need to make a midcourse correction. Be willing to stop and turn 180 degrees, if that is what's called for. It is very important that you be open to correction and that you do not let a bad choice go too long before correcting it.

Avoid the trap of feeling guilty if you do make a wrong turn. Even if no one else accuses you, you may sense a feeling of guilt for making a wrong choice. Don't accept that accusation. It is not from God. *"Forget the former things; do not dwell on the past."* Isaiah 43:18. Concentrate on the future and continue to move toward the second chance that God is giving you. Especially when you fail to hear God clearly and make a wrong choice, be teachable.

"He whose ear listens to the life-giving reproof will dwell among the wise. He who neglects discipline despises himself, but he who listens to reproof acquires understanding. The fear of the Lord is the instruction for wisdom, and before honor comes humility." (Proverbs 15:31-33)

Use the opportunities to learn about your relationship with God, and discern His voice. Learn how to use God's Word more effectively to determine His direction. Learn about yourself and the call or purpose that God has given you. Learn about those around you: who to avoid and who you can turn to for godly advice. Yielding to God, asking advice from trusted brothers and sisters in the Lord, studying His Word, and being willing to surrender or adjust in order to keep His commands and instructions will offer protection from our natural instincts and knee-jerk reactions in life.

Develop Your Plan to Evaluate Choices
Start with a prayer similar to this:

Heavenly Father, I come to You seeking the wisdom which You have promised us in your Word. I thank You for the wisdom and insight that You will grant me through Your Spirit concerning (specific request). Give me discernment to hear Your voice above all others.

By Your authority, I bind the voice of the Enemy, my human logic, and any other voices of this world that would seek to confuse and confound me. May Your will and purpose for my life be fulfilled.

Guide me to understand Your perfect will so that I may discover the best choice that You have for me. I yield to You and to Your will in my life.

In Jesus' name, I pray, Amen

Get into God's Word:

- Start by opening the Bible and read wherever it is that God leads you.
- Find a devotional at a Christian book store or online and use it daily.

Where can you get help to find what you are looking for in God's Word? Check online or at a Christian bookstore or library for:

- Concordance – an index of specific words used in the Bible and where to find them;
- Topical concordance – an index of subjects in the Bible (hope, grace, fear, etc.) and where to find scriptures about them;
- Transliteration tools (material that helps provide definition and context based on original languages such as Hebrew and Greek). Examples include Zodhiates, Vines, and Strong's references which can be found libraries and bookstores.
- And commentaries (insights from knowledgeable theologians) – also available on the internet or in Christian bookstores and libraries.

Other tools include:

- Journaling – to go with your prayer time and study of the Word (this is an excellent tool to help discern the voices you hear and keep track of the things you have heard)
- Fasting – for the purpose of causing you to focus on your requests, your needs, and God's responses.

Know your counselors and those with whom you consult:

- Find and develop a relationship with a godly mentor;
- Cultivate godly friendships;
- Get involved in Christ-based small groups or support groups.

This outline is designed to aid you, but you must invest the time and the effort to follow through. If you do, God will be faithful and will give you an answer. If you listen, He will always tell you what is best for you. That is His promise!

For Discussion/Reflection:

- Have you ever taken an opportunity in your life that turned out to be a distraction?
- If so, how did you know it was a distraction, and what did you do about it?
- If you are facing an opportunity, do you see it as a way to move forward toward your calling or to get away from your loss and pain?
- How does your opportunity line up with what God is saying to you (His Word)?
- What do your godly friends and mentors think about this opportunity? Did you have to "sell" the idea to them, or were they readily in agreement?

Prayer to Discern Between God's Opportunities and Distractions

Heavenly Father, I know that I do not have all the answers. My motives are not always pure. Help me, I pray, by Your Holy Spirit to discern the difference between Your second chances for me and false opportunities. Help me to keep my focus on You and your calling so I can overcome the temptation to run away from pain without healing. Make me teachable so that I will bring You glory as I embrace Your opportunity for me and find success and blessing in becoming the person You designed me to be. In Jesus' name, Amen.

CHAPTER TEN

A "GO" FOR LAUNCH

We live in Florida, within 25 miles of Kennedy Space Center. What the rest of the world stops and watches with wonder has become almost routine for us. We take in stride the roar of the rocket booster engines that rattle the windows in all of the buildings as they propel large rockets into orbit; the piercing light of a night launch that turns darkness into almost-daylight brilliance; the loud, double-crack of the sonic booms as the former Space Shuttle and now the Space X boosters hurtle back through the atmosphere to land on the earth.

The sights and sounds of the launches are just part of the culture. With all of the engineers and other space workers comes a particular jargon – the vernacular of government acronyms and launch verbiage. To a non-technical person, most of it sounds like a foreign language, but one phrase is clear: "Go for launch!"

This phrase is what everything else builds toward. Without it, all of the efforts to achieve the goal of putting the rocket and its payload into space come to a halt.

This phrase must be repeated by each lead person for every system associated with the rocket before the launch can proceed; otherwise, the launch is put on hold – or, even worse, it is aborted. Even non-technical visitors can sense the tension prior to a launch as they wait to hear if everyone signs off on the readiness of their system. And there are goosebumps when those words are repeated one final time … and then, "We are *go* for launch … 10, 9, 8, 7, 6, 5, 4, 3, 2, 1, we have LIFTOFF!"

In the same way, there is both great trepidation and great anticipation at the prospect of finally being ready to launch into your second chance. Some second chances have taken years to get to the place where you are *go* for launch. Other opportunities have come more quickly, but not without the effort to prepare to make the most of each one.

Integral to each second chance – just as with each rocket launch – is purpose. There is no point in launching a rocket just to get it to space; there is always a goal to accomplish. Moreover, the purpose determines the direction of the launch. So it is with our second chances. Without understanding their purpose, there will be no sense of direction or way to measure success.

To understand the purpose of our second chance, we must first know that we have a purpose. At the heart of understanding our purpose are these three truths:

- Even though God may not have inflicted our first loss on us, He can and will use it for both our good and the good of others.
- Learning to assess and apply our experiences to help others will change our entire perspective and approach to our second chance.
- We must identify what our personal second chance is and put a plan together to maximize the opportunity.

Lessons from Peter's Second Chance

Much emphasis is placed on Peter's denial of Jesus just before Christ's crucifixion. Even people who know very little about the Bible are familiar with the part of the story where Peter swore he would stand next to Jesus even to the point of death, but denied his relationship with Jesus three times in the courtyard of the High Priest the night Jesus was arrested. (What made matters worse for

Peter was that Jesus had predicted his failure.) But what happened a few hours earlier and then a few days later tells the most important part of the story.

If all we see is Peter's failure, then we have missed the point completely. Even if we see it as a lesson in grace – Jesus forgave Peter after His resurrection – we fall short of the lesson we are to learn. If we don't hear all of the words Jesus spoke to Peter when He predicted his failure or the word He spoke to Peter after His resurrection, we lose out on the greatest lesson to all of us who face a second chance.

> To understand the purpose of our second chance, we must first know that we have a purpose.

When Jesus prophesied that Peter would deny Him three times, He also prophesied that Peter would be forgiven and given a second chance. And along with that second chance, Jesus would give Him purpose:

> "Simon, Simon, Satan has asked to sift all of you as wheat. But I have prayed for you, Simon, that your faith may not fail. And when you have turned back, strengthen your brothers." (Luke 22:31-32)

Though Peter may have been too distraught to remember Christ's commission at the time of the resurrection, Jesus repeated and enlarged the commission when they met up at the Sea of Galilee later:

> "When they had finished eating, Jesus said to Simon Peter, 'Simon son of John, do you love me more than these?' 'Yes, Lord,' he said, 'you know that I love you.' Jesus said, 'Feed my lambs.' Again Jesus said, 'Simon son of John, do you love me?' He answered, 'Yes, Lord, you know that I love you.' Jesus said, 'Take care of my sheep.' The third time he said to him, 'Simon son of John, do you love me?' Peter was hurt because Jesus asked him the third time, 'Do you love me?' He said, 'Lord, you know all things; you know

that I love you.' Jesus said, 'Feed my sheep.'" (John 21:15-17)

What do we learn from Peter's second chance?

First of all, we will go through trials. There is no getting around it. We will all have to face struggles and problems. Jesus predicted both Peter's failure and his restoration. His words were both a warning and a promise:

> "In this world, you will have trouble. But take heart! I have overcome the world." (John 16:33b)

Many of our problems are simply the result of a fallen world. There are consequences of imperfection and living in the presence of sin which all of us will face in our lives. But we also learn that the Enemy desires to cause us to fail.

Satan would love nothing more than to break us. Understand that although Satan may be afraid of *what God will do* through us, he is not afraid of *us*. His desire is to cause us to fail in order to separate us from God. His desire is to hurt God.

We will fail at times. Satan can "make us" fail. That is why God limits Satan's power and authority. But when we do, we should remember the rest of the promise and the lesson that we learned from Peter: Jesus intercedes for us.

Jesus told Peter, "...*But I have prayed for you, Simon, that your faith may not fail.*" Jesus did not leave Peter to "fend for himself" but He prayed for his strengthening. And He prayed with confidence! The same promise is given to us:

> "Therefore, he is able to save completely those who come to God through Him, because he always lives to intercede for them." (Hebrews 7:25)

We have hope because we do not face our failures alone. Before we even suffered our "lost first," Jesus was already interceding for us and preparing us for our second chance.

Jesus' prayers for us are effective. In the same way Jesus knew the outcome of His prayers for Peter, He also has the same effectiveness for us. "...And *when* you (plural; all; that includes us) have returned...." Despite what Satan will do, our God is more powerful.

"...if God be for us, who can be against us?" (Romans 8:31)

Jesus has overcome the world on our behalf; therefore, we can have confidence that He will overcome our lost firsts. And this paves the way to our future.

The key to finding your purpose is using what you have learned to help others. This gives meaning, not only to our lost first, but also to life itself. Jesus specifically spoke into Peter that he should use the grace he was given to encourage and strengthen his fellow disciples. He took this even further with the commissioning of Peter specifically to "feed My sheep." Three times Jesus challenged Peter: "...do you love Me?" using a Greek form of love that is deep and unconditional. No doubt it countered the doubt Peter must have felt because of his own failure, but it also stretched him to a deeper relationship than he had probably ever thought possible.

The same is true for us. When we face our second chance, we should know that Christ may well challenge us to understand Him in a deeper way than we ever knew was possible. You may have to face the very loss that broke you, so that Christ can help you overcome it. And in all of this, know that you can be victorious, like Peter, in your second chance.

Repurposing of Joseph

Peter was not the Bible's only example of someone whose purpose came out of his lost first. Joseph, the son of Jacob in the Old Testament, is a very important example of how God works through lost firsts to shape us for our second chance. Although Peter's lost first was the result of his personal failure, Joseph's lost first was handed to him by his brothers and other people in his life. Joseph's life teaches us much about what God does through our losses to prepare us for our future. It is a story of "repurposing."

Joseph's story is found in Genesis chapter 37 and in chapters 39-45. We see much more than his actions; we see his values and character. To summarize it as briefly as possible: Joseph was the favorite son of Jacob, which made his eleven brothers angry and jealous. This jealously ultimately resulted in their decision to kill him. They changed their minds and sold him into slavery in Egypt instead. The result was devastating to both his father (and later to his brothers who would come to regret their actions).

Joseph had God's favor on him and was blessed in what he did in Potiphar's service as a slave in Egypt. He grew to the highest level possible in his work. Joseph was also handsome. Potiphar's wife took notice and desired to have an affair with him. Joseph's godly convictions would not allow him to do this, and he denied her. Out of spite, she falsely accused Joseph of attempted rape. He was thrown into prison.

> When we face our second chance, we should know that Christ may well challenge us to understand Him in a deeper way than we ever knew was possible.

While in prison, Joseph once again rose to the top because of God's favor on him, and he was also blessed with a special gift – the ability to interpret dreams.

He interprets the dreams of two servants of the Pharaoh who had also been imprisoned. One dream predicted the man's death and the other's dream predicted his return to service to the Pharaoh. Some years later, Pharaoh himself had a dream that perplexed him. When no one could interpret it, the servant who had been imprisoned with Joseph told the Pharaoh about Joseph. Pharaoh shared his dream with Joseph, who interpreted it as a warning of seven years of good crops, followed by seven years of famine.

In response to Joseph's wisdom and the favor God had placed on him, Pharaoh put Joseph in charge of all preparations for the upcoming famine. Joseph became the second most powerful man in all of Egypt, and most of the Middle East. Following Joseph's instructions, Egypt stored enough extra grain during the good years to feed the entire region during the famine.

The famine forced Joseph's brothers to go to Egypt to purchase grain so their families would not starve. When they arrived, they did not recognize Joseph, although he recognized them. Once again God's character shines through; Joseph has pity on them and does not seek revenge. He does not reveal himself immediately. Instead, he tests them over a period of time, sending them several times between Egypt and Canaan to find out if they are still the same, or if they too have become Godlier in their character. When he sees they are willing to sacrifice themselves for each other and for their family, he finally reveals himself to them and welcomes them into his home.

When he reveals himself to his brothers and they ask for his forgiveness, Joseph states a critical biblical truth:

> "And now, do not be distressed and do not be angry with yourselves for selling me here, because it was to save lives that God sent me ahead of you. For two years now there has been famine in the land, and for the next five years there will be no plowing and reaping. But God sent me ahead of you to preserve for you a remnant on earth and to save your lives by a great deliverance. So then, it was not you who sent me here, but God. He made me father to Pharaoh, lord of his entire household and ruler of all Egypt." (Genesis 45:5-8)

> "But Joseph said to them, 'Don't be afraid. Am I in the place of God? You intended to harm me, but God intended it for good to accomplish what is now being done, the saving of many lives.'" (Genesis 50:19-20)

What happens to us is in God's hands. It is easy to become bitter and defeated by our current situation, but we need to understand that the whole story is not over. God can, has, and will use our circumstances to prepare us for what is to come. Rarely does God let us know in advance of our journey to a particular calling. If we know where we are going, we may opt for shortcuts. We may miss the opportunity for essential preparation by living out each day of our journey. Know that your past and your present will be used for God's future purposes. Trust in His divine providence.

Without a teachable heart, we may fail to learn everything we need to prepare us. Had Joseph not become humble and submissive to God, willing to move beyond anger and self-pity, God could not have raised him up in the new place. If Joseph had become mired in self-pity and depression, he never would have risen to a place of leadership in each of his circumstances. Joseph did not merely "network" through his circumstances; he demonstrated faithful leadership in prison and Potiphar's house. Joseph learned valuable skills each step of the way and, because of the character he exhibited in the face of hardship, he gained the respect of those around him. Ultimately, he stood before the Pharaoh equipped to be a leader of Egypt.

The same is true for you. If you remain depressed and bitter, nothing good will develop in your character, nor will you ever gain the respect of others. On the other hand, if you handle your difficulties and losses as opportunities to exhibit godly character, God will use them to prepare you for your future. The key is to trust the Lord. By so doing, you will be able to embrace your present circumstances as opportunities and remain teachable.

Through crises, we have the opportunity to learn humility. Not much is said about Joseph's flaws, but it is quite possible he was a spoiled child which could breed some issues of pride and arrogance. He was the first son of Jacob's favorite wife Rebecca, who died giving birth to Joseph's younger brother Benjamin. He was a reminder to Jacob of his first love. It would have been difficult for Joseph not to become conceited by all of the special attention.

Regardless of Joseph's background, he learned humility through his experiences. He was reduced to a slave. Then, even after proving his worth, he lost everything due to a lie told about him. His successive hardships prepared him to be the wise leader of an entire country. Slavery and imprisonment were the perfect training grounds for him to break the tendency to operate on his own, as he was repeatedly forced to trust God for the outcome.

In order for us to hear God's voice, we too must surrender to whatever God has for us. Humility is the foundation of teachability. God speaks all the time ... are we listening? Sometimes we may hear Him, but without humility, we will never listen –making what God is saying – irrelevant.

When we are teachable, God is able to rebuild us. In order for God to be able to turn our ashes into beauty we must surrender to Him, wherever we have landed. We can't live in the past. We can't go back; we can't be victims. We must embrace the adventure and opportunity of our present reality. God is a God of healing; He restores what the enemy steals.

> In order for us to hear God's voice, we too must surrender to whatever God has for us. Humility is the foundation of teachability.

Joseph's story is a reminder that forgiveness is crucial for healing and becoming a useful tool for God's plans. We have already spoken about the importance of forgiveness to be ready for a second chance, but I want to take it one step further.

Forgiveness is not just letting go of revenge; it is embracing restoration whenever possible. Joseph was not only willing to forgive his brothers, but he worked to restore his relationship with them. This is not always possible – or even wise when it comes to dangerous situations or people. But wherever prudent, it will serve to strength your role in your second chance.

Finally, be discerning with relationships, opportunities, and applications of your new understanding (wisdom). Joseph had compassion on his brothers, and was generous with their provision, but he was very careful about revealing his identity too soon. We too need to be careful about re-establishing our relationships. We cannot assume that just because we have changed for the better, everyone else we knew has done the same. Whether it is promiscuity, alcoholism, violence, immorality, unethical behavior, or any of the behaviors that may have caused our lost first, becoming reacquainted with those behaviors, or with people who still act them out, will be inviting disaster. We can forgive them, but we cannot bring them back into our lives. If Joseph's brothers had acted the way they did when he was younger, I don't believe that Joseph would have let them back into his life.

Intentional Living

Knowing we have a purpose is important, but it is not the same as living with purpose. Intentional living satisfies our souls. If we have been given a second chance, it is for a reason. Once we have determined the reason, we must be intentional about moving forward in it. I, for one, can relate to the dogs in the Disney Pixar movie "Up." They stayed on task, right up until the moment they spotted a squirrel. Then they would drop everything and chase the squirrel. I can easily become distracted and derailed by the "squirrels" in my life. I start out with good intentions, but when, in the course of my journey, I come across something else that interests me, off I go!

We learned an important lesson regarding this some years ago when an international ministry leader came to our church for a presentation. After the service, we spoke with him about getting involved in international ministry. His answer shocked us and somewhat offended us at the time, but now makes so much more sense. When he determined that our vision was not what his ministry focused on, he redirected us and told us that, with his limited resources, he was unable to invest time into anything that did not further the focus of his ministry. It was disappointing at the time, but today I understand his position. It can become so easy to react to all of the urgent needs around us that we do not ever accomplish the important God-given goal before us.

Intentional living does not mean that you will never be distracted, but by exercising the Spiritual Fruit of self-control, you can learn to recognize when something is a distraction and let it go. Living intentionally means making a choice to stay on task with every aspect of your objective, for the sake of making the most of your second chance. Discernment comes with practice over time, but it is something that all of us can do. It is all about making the choice.

Regardless of what our objective is, I have noticed there are all kinds of choices that go along with intentional living: I need to choose to stay on task; I need to choose to prepare for my purpose; I must get enough sleep; I must get the proper nourishment for my body; I must take time for recreation; and I must especially make time to nourish my spirit. If I'm going to live intentionally and not simply spend my hours responding to urgent needs, I must choose to press into the Holy Spirit every day to gain His wisdom.

We must choose to take care of ourselves – in every aspect of our lives – or we will not be effective with anyone else. If I do not eat well, my blood sugar drops and I begin to be impatient. This leads to me being grouchy (sometimes downright rude and nasty) if I don't have a meal or a snack. At that point, there is no chance for me to give my best to those around me. If I'm weak, weary, and watered down at the end of the day or week, I'm not as likely to effectively invest in others.

Likewise, if I don't spend time with my spouse and/or family for days on end, I become self-concerned and self-driven. I lose the opportunity to be part of a team. I am whole without them, yes, and I have the ability to live independently from them, yes, by all means. But I have chosen to be part of a team. Otherwise, all I am doing is surviving.

The same is true with God. If I have made a choice to become a follower of Jesus, and I fail to spend time with Him and learn of Him, then I fail to live as a light in a dark world. Without Christ, I will miss the opportunities that are all around me. I need to live intentionally when it comes to spending time with Jesus and learning of Him.

Even now, we are learning to use every current life experience to help us understand this material better and to communicate it to others, discovering the best way to use all the pieces of our stories. There are things that each of us bring to the table, and God is blending our experiences into a ministry.

God will use you, your story, your talents, and your skill set to fulfill your purpose. By living intentionally, you will discover not only the lessons that enable you to serve, but also the people to whom God wants you to minister.

Pitfalls and How to Avoid Them

Although we have talked about anger before, it is important to be aware of the danger of embers. These are little thoughts that lie dormant until some piece of your past reappears and brings with it a flood of emotions. For Joseph, it was his brothers turning up in the midst of his new life. Genesis indicates that Joseph was filled with emotion and had to come to terms with it in order to move forward.

Your story and your new opportunity do not come without challenges. There are pitfalls that can cause us to stumble and fall short of the full potential of what God is calling us to do. If we live with the "what if," the "why them," and the "you'll get yours" mindset, we can't be objective and see things with God's view. Without believing we are in His very capable hands, we will be tempted to remain stuck in the mire of "self." It is important that we do not allow any embers to remain that could be fanned back into flame.

Another danger is that of repeating our mistakes. We can be tempted to go back to old habits or addictions. When we are weak and still fragile at heart, we may not be able to withstand temptations, especially those that are triggers for us. Know yourself.

How foolish it would be to stop by a donut shop for a cup of coffee when we are dieting. There are "comfort foods" to be avoided in every aspect of life. We can perpetuate our problems and remain in the same historical cycle if we do not ask God for wisdom and discernment through prayer and choose to avoid those familiar things, those defaults that leave us vulnerable to rolling back into old patterns of behavior.

Beware of the pitfall of reaching out too soon. We discussed earlier in the book the danger of filling emotional gaps in our life without first healing. Now, however, I want to point out the danger, specifically, of moving into ministry too soon. It is possible to have healed from the first loss, but be too new to your second chances to be ready to help others.

> Time for inner healing is essential ... it may be healthy to take our eyes off ourselves and look to serving others.

A year after we got married, we were anxious to use our experience to help others, so we attended a Divorce Care training class. The church was more than eager to have us take a leadership role; however, as we sought God on the matter, we both heard clearly that we needed more time in building our relationship before we could safely use our experience to help others. In our particular case, we were both mature Christians, and we had also healed from our respective crises; however, our new marriage had not matured enough to withstand the spiritual warfare involved in frontline ministry. Therefore, God called us to be patient and work on our marriage; this would be the foundation of our ministry.

Without healing first, your "assistance" to others may only be a way of venting your feelings or deferring your pain. Remember, "fixing" others is not a way to heal yourself. Take care not to fall into a co-dependent relationship. When we are not healthy mentally or spiritually, we cannot truly help others. When we use others to make us feel better, we short-change both parties.

It is critical to focus on healing before we focus on advancing. Take time off from over-involvement in order to deal with personal issues resulting from loss. If we are still contagious, we run the risk of contaminating others. We must use wisdom and discernment in determining when we have healed sufficiently to re-engage in ministry. Ministry involves leadership over others and has a level of responsibility and accountability. The only way to know for sure that you are ready is to ask God for discernment and seek the input of godly people, especially your pastor. If you are honest with others about your concern with your readiness to serve, I'm certain they will be honest in their advice.

On the other hand, while time for inner healing is essential, it may be healthy to take our eyes off ourselves and look to serving others. Serving involves doing things for others, not exercising leadership over others. Taking our eyes off ourselves in order to help others may actually facilitate healing. Think of a sore muscle. Catering to it only creates further stiffness and pain. When we get up and walk, albeit slowly and with discomfort, the result is beneficial. Look for God-given opportunities to help or to serve others.

God's Economy

"God's Economy" is a way to describe the concept that God is perfectly efficient in using every aspect of our lives to help us prepare for and live out our purpose. Although God does not cause everything to happen in our lives, He can and will use everything in our lives. Some things He uses to break old (bad) habits and other things He uses to develop new skills. Let's look at some of the ways God works His economy in our lives:

> In God's economy, no trial or life experience is wasted. Therefore, every experience will be used to fulfill a purpose. Even things we may consider dead and useless in our lives can serve another purpose in God's plan.

Most have seen videos about "lifehacks," which are creative ways to use common items for a different purpose than was originally intended. For example, using paper clamps as cord organizers or covers over razors, turning a broken pot into a faerie garden or other art, using old bicycles to hold potted plants, using contact lens cases as makeup containers.

In a much greater way, God uses the common experiences of our lives and even the lost or dead elements of our lost first to prepare us for our second chances. In my lost first career in ministry, I thought that evangelism and preaching were "dead" skills, with no application in a secular job. Nevertheless, those were the very skills I needed (in a different form) to be successful as a financial developer, salesman, and consultant. Just because those skills were originally intended for ministry did not mean they had no other applications. In the same way, there are elements of relationships, personal management, and wisdom that can be salvaged from your previous experiences and used in your second chance. Don't make the mistake of thinking that God cannot use you and all of your experience just because you can't see how at this time.

God uses our life experience to change our personal direction. As we have said, God loves us despite who we are, but He also loves us enough not to leave us there. He purposes to change our personal direction. God builds on what we have already learned, what we are currently learning, and what we will learn in the future.

Through our struggles, God can redirect us back to our first love. He can reacquaint us with the very character traits He originally gave us. Our "setbacks" may be blessings, even though we don't see them that way at the time.

Sometimes God's economy protects us from dangers we don't see. Some of the losses we have experienced may actually have saved us from greater losses. The break up with a boyfriend or girlfriend may have spared us a troubled marriage or even a divorce. A lost job can prevent us from being in a compromising position. The list could go on, but the point is that God may use your lost first to prevent you from experiencing a greater – or even worse – a permanent loss.

God's economy makes use of our struggles to perfect our character.

"And not only this, but we also exult in our tribulations, knowing that tribulation brings about perseverance; 4and perseverance, proven character; and proven character, hope; 5and hope does not disappoint, because the love of God has been poured out within our hearts through the Holy Spirit who was given to us." (Romans 5:3-5)

Remember that your character is so much more important than your accomplishments. The age-old definition of character stands true: "Character is who you are and what you do when no one else is looking." Our trials help to shape who we are and the decision we make. The trials may not be a critical step in giving us a second chance, but they can lay the foundation for us to make wise, godly decisions that will make our second chance successful.

God's economy enables us to use our experiences to help others who are struggling. While you do not have to personally experience everything to be able to encourage others, there is no question that, having gone through a similar set of trials, you have insight into both the logistics of a struggle and the emotions of a struggle. It may be easier for others to open up and share their situation with you because you have gone through something similar to their experience.

> Look to be an encourager. You have reason for it, and others need it, every single day.

Sometimes a lack of common experience can lead to judgmental criticism. The result is that people frequently hesitate to share their hurts or needs. This is why your experience can be so valuable in God's economy. Think back to your own crises. Who did you turn to? Who were your mentors? Lest anybody say, "my story is not that important," know that you may be the one God is counting on to reach the people He brings into your life.

In God's economy, our pain can become the asset of empathy. Personal experience can make us more sensitive to and understanding of people who are facing the same thing. We may be able to be more patient with them or to know when they are getting stuck in the process.

Finding Our Role in Other People's Second Chances

Peter was called to use his experience to encourage others, and we also may be called to use our experience to help others heal. But more than just healing, we may play a critical role in their post-recovery opportunities. You may be able to help others launch into a ministry of second chances.

Even if you do not have a calling to help those who need a second chance, you do have a ministry. There will be many opportunities to love and help others, but you will be more attuned to those needing encouragement in the area of your first loss. Even if you do not counsel them further, encouraging them toward their second chance will empower them.

Encouragement can take the form of acknowledging others' gifts and potential as well as valuing who they are. There are enough voices that will say what they cannot do, but if you remain focused on what God has done for you, you can be a voice of hope. We can even encourage them by simply avoiding the tendency to label them by their lost first. The world will be more than eager to put them in a box just like the world tried to do to you. But you know the truth. Speak the truth of their self-worth through Christ Jesus and you will make a dramatic difference in their lives and successful second chances.

The Bible teaches us that God sees us as we can be through Christ Jesus, and if we see others through the eyes of God, we can do the same. Treat them with all respect as though they are capable of everything they need to be to fulfill their second chance. How we react to a person can help them believe in themselves and their future.

Your role in helping someone else with their second chance may require the courage to love them by saying "no" or abstaining from intervention. There will be plenty of others to tell them that they are a failure. There will also be plenty of others to tell them what they want to hear, regardless of whether or not it is good for them. With your experience and prayer, you can be a voice of truth, even by saying "no."

Lastly, we must avoid the temptation to keep fixing others' problems, which can actually prevent them from ever overcoming them. In showing understanding, we must be careful not to handicap another person's chances of healing. Although it may be critical to offer encouragement, we don't want to retard their growth by removing their opportunity to learn and grow.

Science has taught us this lesson in nature. After watching how difficult it was for a chicken to hatch from its egg, scientists helped the chick break free. The result surprised the observers. The chick failed to thrive and ultimately died. The same was true for a butterfly which was assisted in hatching from its cocoon. What was the lesson? The strength gained by each of these creatures as each broke free from its old life was essential for it to thrive in its new life. Without the struggle, it lacked the strength needed to survive in its new environment.

We may think we are helping, but it is in the struggle that the person learns to overcome and develop. It may be tempting to fix a situation that you have previous experience with; however, it may be far more compassionate in the end to allow them to make their own choice and face the consequences. Your role, nevertheless, remains to be an encourager.

It's Your Turn Now
Once you are "'go" for launch, ask yourself these questions:

- What lessons have I learned?
- How can I use what I've learned to make a difference in someone else's life?
- What am I doing to make the most of my second chances?

- How is God repurposing me?

In the same way that God has blessed us, we know that He will bless you as well. He is a God of Second Chances, and most often a God of Many Chances. We hope the subjects discussed in this book will inspire you as much as they did us and empower you for your future.

Recorded in the book of Matthew just before Jesus returned to Heaven, Christ's Great Commission was "…Go, and make disciples of all nations, … teaching them everything I have commanded you … and I will be with you to the very end of the age." A ministry of second chances is a ministry of discipleship. This is a commission for you.

It is our prayer that God would bless you in your second chance, that you would have an anointing of the Holy Spirit to discern what God is doing in your life and what you need to do to walk in His will.

We ask, Lord, that You would bless the reader of this book with strength and courage to walk out their second chance, and that You would repurpose them according to Your will. Use their faithfulness to enlarge their territory for Your Kingdom's sake. We pray that they will grow in grace and You will use them to impact the lives of others.

May they be blessed with a successful second chance, and may they find purpose in life that was previously missing! To You, Oh Lord, be all the glory. In Jesus Name!